Catches and Rounds

MUSIC ALONE SHALL LIVE

1. All things shall per - ish from un - der the sky.

2. Mu - sic a - lone shall live, Mu - sic a - lone shall live,

3. Mu - sic a - lone shall live, Nev - er to die.

SONG IN AMERICA

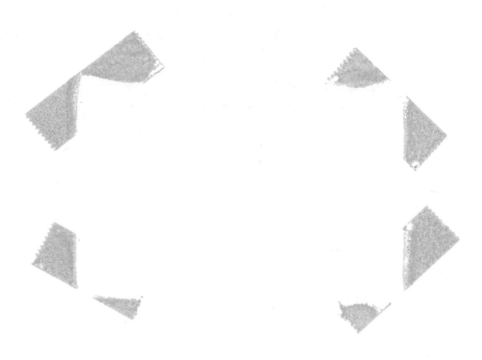

Books by Burl Ives

WAYFARING STRANGER

TALES OF AMERICA

SAILING ON A VERY FINE DAY

THE BURL IVES SONG BOOK

SEA SONGS

IRISH SONGS

MAJOR, MACK AND BURLY JIM-BOVO

A WAYFARER'S NOTEBOOK

SONG IN AMERICA

BURL IVES

Song in America

OUR MUSICAL HERITAGE

Arrangements by Albert Hague

NEW YORK

DUELL, SLOAN AND PEARCE

ACKNOWLEDGMENTS

I wish there were an adequate way to say thank you to all the people in audiences, everywhere, who have heartened me and my belief in the beauty of these songs. I wish to thank the many people who have brought me the songs of their parents and grandparents, so that my knowledge of the folksongs of America could be as full as possible. I wish, in particular, of course, to thank the Lomaxes and the great collectors, to whom all of us interested in this field, singers and academicians, owe so much. My thanks to MacKinlay Kantor, whose feeling for the songs of America is unequaled and whose knowledge of them is extensive. My gratitude to Ralph Satz, editor extraordinaire, and devoted musician Albert Hague, who has so ably captured the quality of these songs on the piano, for which they were not originally intended. And to my wife, Helen Ives, for her devotion to the cause of folk music. Last but not least, I certainly wish to thank Florence Sharkstein for her devoted research and attention to the details of this book; without her work we often could not have gone ahead.

I owe particular thanks to MacKinley Kantor for the last two verses of "The Pirate Song" and the last verse of "Brennan on the Moor."

The version of "The Wabash Cannon Ball" is by Burl Ives and Gordon Jenkins.

In addition, my thanks to the following for permission to use their material:

Leeds Music Corporation for: "The Blue Tail Fly"; arranged by Burl Ives; © MCMXLIV, MCMXLV by Leeds Music Corporation, New York, New York; reprinted by permission; all rights reserved. "The Cowboy's Lament"; arranged by Burl Ives; © MCMXLV, MCMXLVI, MCMXLIX by Leeds Music Corporation, New York, New York; reprinted by permission; all rights reserved. "Big Rock Candy Mountain"; words and music arranged by Burl Ives; © MCMLVII by Leeds Music Corporation, New York, New York; reprinted by permission; all rights reserved. "The Foggy, Foggy Dew"; arranged by Burl Ives; © MCMXLV by Leeds Music Corporation, New York, New York; reprinted by permission; all rights reserved.

Southern Music for the following from their folio *Children's Songs:* "The Maid of Amsterdam," "Hush Little Baby," "Three Jolly Huntsmen," "Let's Go A-Hunting," "The Crocodile Song," "Mister Rabbit," "The Whale," "Buckeye Jim"; and for the following from their folio, *Folksongs and Ballads:* "St. John's River (Baby, Did You Hear?)," "Goober Peas," "I Know Where I'm Going," "Lavender Cowboy," "Leather-Winged Bat," "Lolly Too-Dum Day," "Old Blue," "Old Paint," "Skip to My Lou."

The performance rights for all other songs in this book are copyrighted by Wayfarer Music Co., Inc.

Affiliate of
MEREDITH PRESS
Des Moines & New York

CONTENTS

PREFACE

This book reflects the spirit and some of the experiences of America told musically. In this backlog of American song is a common wealth, giving us subject matter as varied as the interests of men, reflecting tragedy and comedy in memorable words and melody, telling of local events and national, of men working, sailing, and marching, living communally and alone. They are songs with a content of fun or tragedy or gentleness whose captivating melodies make them a memorable joy to sing.

By dramatizing, and making personally vivid, events that would otherwise be schoolbook episodes, folk songs are creating real and well-based pride in America's past and present. This may be their most important function today, together with the fact that through recordings and short-wave broadcasts they are winning admiration for native American folk music abroad.

Folk songs created in singers the spirit which generated them. They can be sung by anyone who has imagination and can carry a melody. Sung by an individual they enrich his life, sung by groups they create a spirit of unity, and from this unity inevitably comes a sense of belonging.

More and more this American heritage of songs is becoming the basis for music in the schools, is sung by camp groups, in the homes and in the colleges. These songs are our shared heritage, and when the people of a country sing them together, it can only strengthen their national bonds.

Passed down from generation to generation, the songs in this book exist in many versions. What version is to be sung is a matter of poetic and musical taste. Of course, the songs in this book reflect my taste, but since they are versions of songs often sung today, I feel justified in presenting them as I sing them.

Years ago, when I felt my purpose in life was to help make these songs known to the American public, I had to make decisions. I never felt that songs from the past were good because they were out of the past. The past has its proportion of bad melodies and bad ideas just as today has. I decided the origin of a song was of academic value only, compared to longevity and use. If a song could be sung, if its meaning came through, if its melody tripped the tongue and caught at the heart, if it communicated, if it could be enjoyed, that meant it was worth everything I could give it.

Identifying myself with the minstrel of old, I took his traditional liberty. Sometimes I sang a song as I found it; often I worked on its content and music to make the melody and meaning what I felt was its fullest expression.

A book, like a picture, has a definite limit and size. I regret that problems of space have made me leave out many songs. However, I do think you will find in this section an exceptionally large number of the American heritage of songs, and I hope you will enjoy singing them as much as I do.

OUR SONG INHERITANCE

Song in America began with the colonists who brought over their music, sacred and secular, along with their guns, clothes, and basic provisions. These early settlers were Dutch, German, and French, as well as British, but English was the immediately accepted language of the colonies. English literature became the foundation of our culture, all others becoming embodied in it. Dutch and French songs gradually lost currency, while the English traditional song was transmitted from person to person, from parent to child, to grandchild.

It will help us to appreciate what these songs were and are if we look back for a moment to these times. The colonists, at least for the first generation or two, were away from home, not members of another nation, and so their songs were songs of England or Europe. They sang from words scribbled in the dog-eared pages of their commonplace books, from hymnals and song books. They sang songs carried in the memory, humming or singing around the fire or at work, songs learned in childhood and later passed on to their children.

We should remember, too, that people in those days, both in England and in the colonies, sang much more for their own pleasure than we do now. The more educated learned to read music at sight. They gathered at one another's houses to sing rounds and madrigals. In the taverns or on shipboard, wherever men entertained themselves, it was usual for someone to tell a story in song or sing verses, which others joined in the chorus.

Ships brought over friends, relatives, goods for exchange, news—and current songs. These songs, whether current on sea or land, took all possible forms: rounds, chanties, song stories (the narrative ballads); songs of love, courtship, and marriage; children's games and lullabies.

Until very recently, the old songs were known only in small areas in isolated parts of our country. They were handed down within a family circle or to a small group. There was no way for them to become known over the whole country; they were not really a part of everyone's heritage or the nation's general culture. They became known first when collectors and researchers became interested in these songs, and then as they were heard nationally over the radio. Finally, through educational projects in the schools, we find this musical heritage, with songs of American origin, becoming a part of every schoolchild's experience.

THE TAILOR AND THE MOUSE

Lively, in 2

There was a tai - lor had a mouse, Hi - did - dle dum cum
The tai - lor had a tall silk hat, Hi - did - dle dum cum
The tai - lor he chased him o - ver the lea, Hi - did - dle dum cum

feed - a   They lived to - geth - er in one house.
feed - a   The mouse he ate it, fan - cy that.
feed - a   The last of that mouse he never did see.

Hi did - dle dum cum feed - a.   Hi did - dle dum, cum

tin-trum, tan-trum, through the town of Ram-sey,—

Hi did-dle dum, come o-ver the lea,

Hi did-dle dum cum feed-a. ____

3

THREE JOLLY HUNTSMEN

Fast - in 2

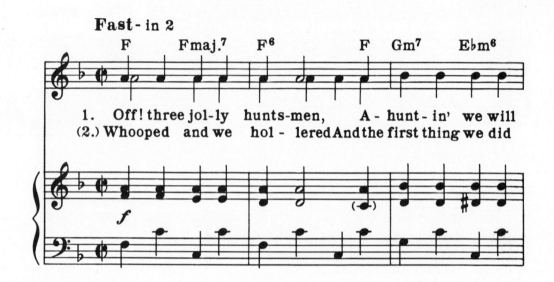

1. Off! three jol-ly hunts-men, A - hunt-in' we will
(2.) Whooped and we hol - lered And the first thing we did

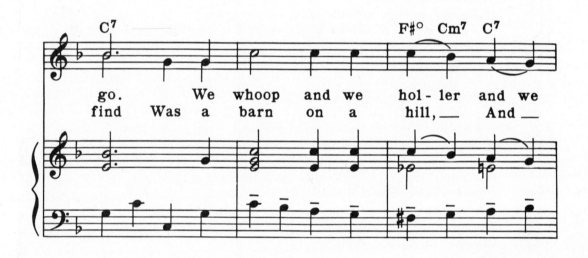

go. We whoop and we hol - ler and we
find Was a barn on a hill, And

blow our horns al - so. Look-y there now!
that we left be - hind. Look-y there now!

3. We whooped and we hollered and the next thing we did find:
Was a bull calf in a pen and that we left behind. Looky there, now.
One said it was a bull calf, one said "Nay,"
One said a painted jackass that has never learnt to bray.
    Looky there, now.

4. We whooped and we hollered and the next thing we did find:
Were some children leaving school and these we left behind.
    Looky there, now.
One said that they were children, one said "Nay,"
One said they're only little angels, we'll leave them to their play.
    Looky there, now.

5. We whooped and we hollered and the next thing we did find:
A fat pig in a ditch and that we left behind. Looky there, now.
One said it was a pig, one said "Nay,
A politician with his clothes stole away." Looky there, now.

6. We whooped and we hollered and the next thing we did find:
A frog in a well; him we left behind. Looky there, now.
One said it was a frog, one said "Nay,"
One said it was a jay-bird with the feathers plucked away.
    Looky there, now.

7. We whooped and we hollered and the next thing we did find:
The moon in the trees; that we left behind. Looky there, now.
One said it was the moon, one said "Nay,"
One said it was a cheese with a half cut away. Looky there, now.

8. We whooped and we hollered and the next thing we did find:
Two lovers in the lane; these we left behind. Looky there, now.
One said they were two lovers, one said "Nay,"
One said two wanderin' lunatics, let them go their way.
    Looky there, now.

9. We whooped and we hollered and the next thing we did find:
An owl in the tree and that we left behind. Looky there, now.
One said it was an owl, one said "Nay,"
One said it was a ghost and we all ran away. Looky there, now.

10. So we whooped and we hollered past the setting of the sun,
An there's naught to bring away, now hunting day is done.
    Looky there, now.
So we one unto the other said, "This hunting doesn't pay,
But we've prowled up and down a bit and had a rattling day."
    Looky there, now.

PRETTY POLLY

With a steady beat

I court-ed pret-ty Pol - ly the live - long night, I court-ed pret-ty Pol - ly the live - long night, then left her next morn-ing be - fore it was light.

2. "Pretty Polly, pretty Polly, come go along with me,
   Pretty Polly, pretty Polly, come go along with me
   Before we get married some pleasures to see."

3. She jumped on behind him and away they did go;
   She jumped on behind him and away they did go
   Over the hills and the valley below.

4. They went a little further and what did they spy;
   They went a little further and what did they spy,
   A new dug grave with a spade laying by.

5. "Oh, Willie, oh, Willie, I'm 'fraid of your way;
   Oh, Willie, oh, Willie, I'm 'fraid of your way;
   I'm afraid you will lead my poor body astray."

6. "Pretty Polly, pretty Polly, you've guessed about right;
   Pretty Polly, pretty Polly, you've guessed about right;
   For I slept on your grave the best part of last night."

7. He throwed her on the ground and she broke into tears;
   He throwed her on the ground and she broke into tears;
   She throwed her arms around him and trembled with fear.

8. There's no time to talk now, there's no time to stand;
   There's no time to talk now, there's no time to stand;
   He drew out his knife all in his right hand.

9. He stabbed her in the heart and the blood it did flow;
   He stabbed her in the heart and the blood it did flow,
   And into the grave pretty Polly did go.

10. He put on a little dirt and he started for home;
    Throwed on a little dirt and he started for home,
    Leaving no one behind but the wild birds to moan.

11. A debt to the devil Willie must pay;
    A debt to the devil Willie must pay;
    For killing pretty Polly and running away.

THE SAILOR'S RETURN

1. As I walked out one sum-mer's eve-ning
2. I stepped up to her and kind-ly asked her

To take the cool and pleas-ant air, 'Twas
If she would be a poor sail-or's wife, "Oh,

there I spied a fine, young la - dy And she
no, kind sir, I don't want to mar - ry, I'd

looked to me ____ like a li - ly fair. _____
rath - er live ____ a sin - gle life." _____

3. "What makes you so far from all human nature?
    What makes you so far from womankind?
    You are young, you are fair and handsome;
    You can marry me if you're so inclined."

4. "The truth, kind sir, I'll plainly tell you:
    I could have been married three years ago
    To one John Reilly, who left this country;
    He's been the cause of my grief and woe."

5. "Don't think upon Reilly and do forget him
    And go with me to a distant shore,
    And we will sail to Pennsylvany;
    Adieu to Reilly forever more."

6. "I'll not go with you to Pennsylvany,
    I won't go with you to a distant shore;
    For my heart is with Reilly and I can't forget him,
    Although I may never see him more."

7. Now when he saw that she loved him truly,
    He gave her kisses one, two, three,
    Saying, "I am Reilly, your long lost lover,
    Who's been the cause of your misery."

8. "If you be he and your name is Reilly,
    I'll go with you to a distant shore;
    We'll sail all over to Pennsylvany;
    Adieu, young friends, forevermore."

BRENNAN ON THE MOOR

Free in delivery, with mounting excitement

1. It's a - bout a fierce high-way man my sto - ry I will
2. It was up - on the King's high-way old Bren-nan he sat

tell. His name was Wil - ly Bren-nan, and in
down. He met the mayor of Moor-land five

Ire - land he did dwell. 'Twas up - on the King's_
miles out - side of town. Now the May - or, he knew

mountain he began his wild career, and
Brennan, and, "I think," says he, "your

many a rich gentleman before him shook with fear. Oh, it's
name is Willy Brennan, you must come along with me." Oh, it's

CHORUS: steady, like a dirge

Brennan on the moor, Brennan on the moor,

slower

bold, gay, and undaunted stood young Brennan on the moor.

slower

3. Now Brennan's wife was a-going down town
Some provisions for to buy.
When she saw her Willy taken
She began to weep and cry.
Says he, "Hand me that ten penny,"
And as soon as Willy spoke
She handed him a blunderbuss
From underneath her cloak.
            Chorus

4. Now Brennan got his blunderbuss,
My story I'll unfold.
He caused the mayor to tremble
And to deliver up his gold.
Five thousand pounds were offered
For his apprehension there,
But Brennan and the pedlar
To the mountain did repair.
            Chorus

5. Now Brennan is an outlaw
All on some mountain high.
With infantry and cavalry
To take him they did try,
But he laughed at them and he scorned at them
Until it was said
By a false-hearted woman
He was cruelly betrayed.
            Chorus

6. They hung Brennan at the crossroads;
In chains he swung and dried.
But still they say that in the night
Some do see him ride.
They see him with his blunderbuss
In the midnight chill;
Along, along the King's highway
Rides Willy Brennan still.
            Chorus

WALY, WALY
(COCKLE SHELLS)

Slow and free in delivery

When cock - le - shells _____ turn sil - ver bells, _____ Then will my love re - turn to _ me. _____ When ro - ses blow _____ in win - ter

old _____ and wax-eth cold, _____ And fades a-

way like morn - ing dew. _____

TURKISH REVERY

in the low down,___ low___
her in the low down,___ low___

down, low___ down, As she sails in the low down, lone-some
down, low___ down, If you sink her in the low down, lone-some

low?"
low?"

r. h.

p

3. Then he bared his breast and he swam in the tide
   And he bored three holes in the old ship's side.
   He sunk her in the low down, low down, low down,
   He sunk her in the low down, lonesome low.

4. Then he bared his breast and he swam in the tide
   And he swam right back to his own ship's side.
   And she rolled in the low down, low down, low down,
   She rolled in the low down, lonesome low.

5. "Captain, captain, take me on board;
   If you don't, you'll have to forfeit your word,
   For you promised in the low down, low down, low down,
   You promised in the low down, lonesome low."

6. "Sailor boy, sailor boy, don't appeal to me,
   For you drowned fifty souls when you sank the Revery.
   Yes, you drowned them in the low down, low down, low down,
   You drowned them in the low down, lonesome low."

7. "If it wasn't for the love that I hold for your men,
   I'd sink you the same as I sunk them.
   I'd sink you in the low down, low down, low down,
   I'd sink you in the low down, lonesome low."

8. Then he bared his breast and down sank he,
   He sank till he came to the bottom of the sea,
   And he drowned in the low down, low down, low down,
   He drowned in the low down, lonesome low.

LILY MUNRO

With a haunting, soft rhythm

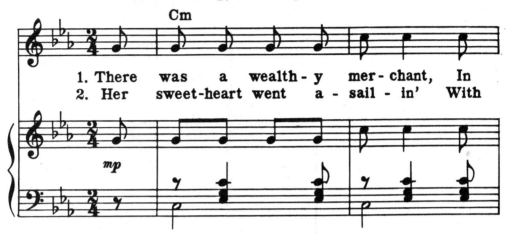

1. There was a wealth-y mer-chant, In
2. Her sweet-heart went a - sail - in' With

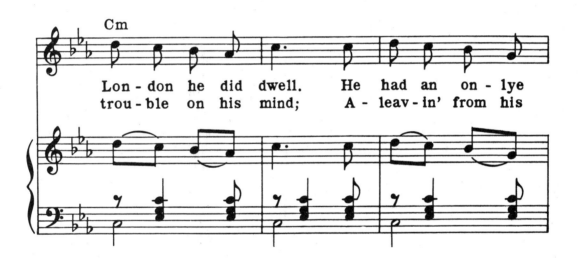

Lon - don he did dwell. He had an on - lye
trou - ble on his mind; A - leav-in' from his

daugh-ter, And the truth to you I'll tell.
coun - try, And his own true love be - hind.

CHORUS:

Lay _____ the Lil-y - o,   Lay _____

the Lil-y - o!

3. This girl she dressed herself all up in man's array,
And to the war department she then did march away.
Lay the Lily-o, lay the Lily-o.

4. "Before you come on board, sir, your name we'd like to know!"
A smile played o'er her countenance. "They call me wee Munro."
Lay the Lily-o, lay the Lily-o.

5. "Your waist is slim and slender, your fingers they are small,
Your cheeks too red and rosy to face a cannon ball."
Lay the Lily-o, lay the Lily-o.

6. "I know my waist is slender, my fingers they are small,
But it would not make me tremble to see ten thousand fall."
Lay the Lily-o, lay the Lily-o.

7. The drum began to beat, the fife began to play,
   And straightway to the battlefield they all did march away.
   Lay the Lily-o, lay the Lily-o.

8. And when the war was ended, this girl she searched the ground
   Among the dead and wounded till her own true love she found.
   Lay the Lily-o, lay the Lily-o.

9. This couple they got married, so well they did agree;
   This couple they got married, so why not you and me?
   Lay the Lily-o, lay the Lily-o.

THE FOGGY, FOGGY DEW

Free in delivery

1. When I was a bach-'lor, I lived all a-lone, I worked at the weav-er's trade; and the on-ly, on-ly thing that I did that was wrong, was to woo a fair young maid. I

2. One night she knelt close by my side when I was fast a-sleep. she threw her arms a-round my neck, and then be-gan to weep. She

3. Again I am a bachelor, I live with my son,
   We work at the weaver's trade;
   And every single time that I look into his eyes,
   He reminds me of the fair young maid.
   He reminds me of the wintertime,
   Part of the summer, too,
   And of the many, many times that I held her in my arms,
   Just to keep her from the foggy, foggy dew.

GREENSLEEVES

CHORUS:

4. I bought thee petticoats of the best,
   The cloth so fine as might be;
   I gave thee jewels for thy chest,
   And all this cost I spent on thee. *Chorus:*

5. Thy smock of silk, both fair and white,
   With gold embroidered gorgeously;
   Thy petticoat of sendal right,*
   And these I bought thee gladly. *Chorus:*

6. They set thee up, they took thee down,
   They served thee with humility;
   Thy foot might not once touch the ground,
   And yet thou wouldst not love me. *Chorus:*

7. Well I will pray to God on high,
   That thou my constancy mayst see,
   And that yet once before I die
   Thou wilt vouchsafe to love me. *Chorus:*

8. Greensleeves, now farewell! adieu!
   God I pray to prosper thee!
   For I am still thy lover true,
   Come once again and love me. *Chorus:*
*Thin silk

I KNOW MY LOVE

In a gay spirit

I know my love __ by her way of walk-ing, And
I know my love __ by her way of talk-ing, And
I know my love __ by her suit of blue. __ But if

boys are few," Yet if my love leaves me, what will I do?

2. There's a dance hall at Malachite
   Where my true love goes every night
   And sits upon some strange lad's knee.
   Well, then, don't you know now, that vexes me.
   Chorus

BILLY BOY

(ENGLISH)

In 2, not too fast

1. Where have you been all the day, my boy Wil-lie?
2. Is she fit to be a wife, my boy Wil-lie?

Where have you been all the day, Wil-lie won't you tell me now?
Is she fit to be a wife, Wil-lie won't you tell me now?

I have been all the day court-in' of a la-dy gay,
She's as fit to be a wife as a fork fits to a knife,

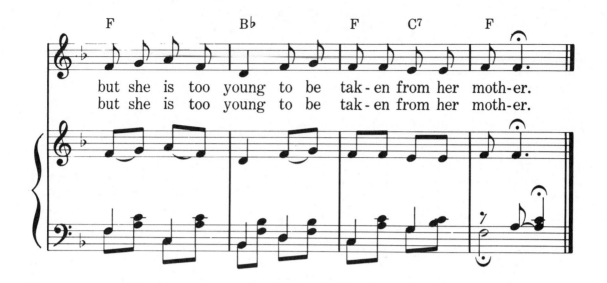

but she is too young to be tak-en from her moth-er.
but she is too young to be tak-en from her moth-er.

3. Can she cook and can she spin, my boy Willie?
   Can she cook and can she spin, Willie won't you tell me now?
   She can cook, she can spin, she can do most anything,
   But she is too young to be taken from her mother.

4. Can she bake a cherry pie, my boy Willie?
   Can she bake a cherry pie, Willie won't you tell me now?
   She can bake a cherry pie, quick's a cat can wink his eye,
   But she is too young to be taken from her mother.

5. Does she often go to church, my boy Willie?
   Does she often go to church, Willie won't you tell me now?
   Yes, she often goes to church in a bonnet white as birch,
   But she is too young to be taken from her mother.

6. Can she make a feather-bed, my boy Willie?
   Can she make a feather-bed, Willie won't you tell me now?
   She can make a feather-bed, and put pillows at the head,
   But she is too young to be taken from her mother.

7. Did she ask you to come in, my boy Willie?
   Did she ask you to come in, Willie will you tell me now?
   Yes, she asked me to come in, she has a dimple in her chin,
   But she is too young to be taken from her mother.

8. Did she tell how old she is, my boy Willie?
   Did she tell how old she is, Willie won't you tell me now?
   She's three times six, seven times seven, twenty-eight and eleven,
   But she is too young to be taken from her mother.

BILLY BOY

(IRISH)

Bright, in 2

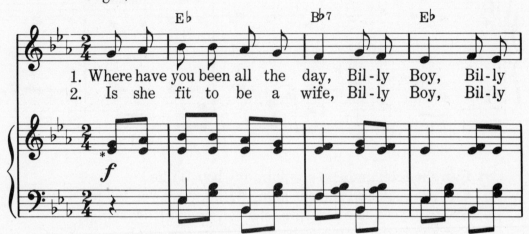

*The repeated E♭ in the right hand is optional.

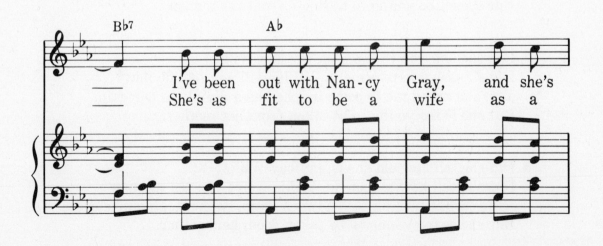

stol-en me heart a - way.— She's me Nan-cy, tick-led me
fork fits to a knife.

fan - cy, oh, me charm-in' Bil - ly Boy.

slower

slower

RAGGLE-TAGGLE GYPSIES

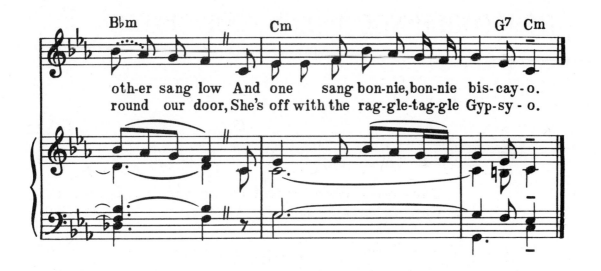

oth-er sang low And one sang bon-nie, bon-nie bis-cay-o.
round our door, She's off with the rag-gle-tag-gle Gyp-sy - o.

3. It was late last night when my Lord came home,
Inquiring for his a-lady-o.
The servants said, in every end,
"She's off with the Raggle-Taggle Gypsy-o."

4. "Go bring to me my milk-white steed
And fetch to me my pony-o,
That I may ride to seek my bride,
Who's off with the Raggle-Taggle Gypsy-o."

5. Then he rode high and he rode low;
He rode over copses and hedges low.
He rode till he came to a wide open field,
And then he a-spied his Lady-o.

6. "What makes you leave your home and green land?
What makes you leave your money-o?
What makes you leave your new-wedded Lord?
To go with the Raggle-Taggle Gypsy-o?"

7. "What care I for my home and land?
What care I for my money-o?
What care I for my new-wedded Lord?
I'm off with the Raggle-Taggle Gypsy-o."

8. "Oh, last night you slept in a goose-feathered bed
With the sheets turned down so bravely-o.
But tonight you shall sleep in the cold open field
Alone with the Raggle-Taggle Gypsy-o."

9. "What care I for your goose-feathered bed
With the sheets turned down so bravely-o?
For tonight I shall sleep in the cold open field
Alone with the Raggle-Taggle Gypsy-o."

HOW COULD YOU USE A POOR MAIDEN SO?

Lyrical

1. Ear - ly one morn-ing, just as the sun was ris - ing, I
2. Gay is the gar - land, and fresh are the ros - es, That

heard   a maid   say-ing in the   val - ley be-low,
'I cut   from my gar - den to   bind in my hair.

"Oh, don't de - ceive me!   Oh, nev-er   leave me!

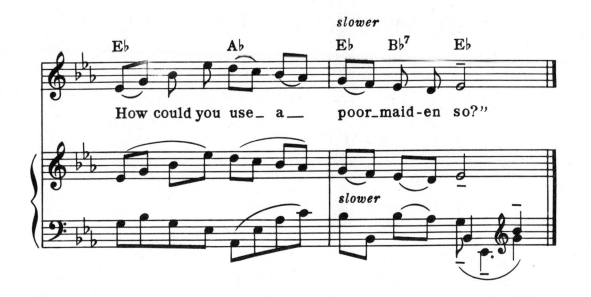

slower

How could you use＿ a＿ poor＿maid-en so?"

3. Thus spoke the fair maiden, her sorrows bewailing,
   Thus spoke the fair maiden in the valley below,
   "Oh, don't deceive me!
   Oh, never leave me!
   How could you use a poor maiden so?"

TWO MAIDENS WENT MILKING

A gentle serenade

1. Two maid - ens went milk - ing one   day. ___
2. They met with a   man they did   know. ___

Two maid - ens went milk - ing one   day. ___
They met with a   man they did   know. ___

And the wind it   did blow high And the wind   it did blow
And they said:"Have you the skill?"And they said:"Have you the

low. And it toss-èd their pails to and fro;
will For to catch us a small bird or two;

And it toss-èd their pails to and fro.
For to catch us a small bird or two?"

3. "Here's a health to the blackbird in the bush,
Likewise the merry merry doe.
If you'll come along with me,
Under yonder flowering tree,
I might catch you a small bird or two;
I might catch you a small bird or two."

4. So they went and they sat 'neath the bush.
They went and they sat 'neath two.
And the birds flew 'round about,
Pretty birds flew in and out,
And he caught them by one and by two;
And he caught them by one and by two.

5. So, my boys, let us drink down the sun.
My boys let us drink down the moon.
Take your lady to the wood,
If you really think you should,
You might catch her a small bird or two;
You might catch her a small bird or two.

THE KEYS TO CANTERBURY

Free in delivery

1. Oh, mad - am, I would give to you the keys of Can - ter -
2. Oh, sir, I shan't ac - cept of you the keys of Can - ter -

bur - y, ___ And all the bells of Lon - don will
bur - y, ___ Nor all the bells of Lon - don won't

ring to make us mer - ry ___ If you will be my
ring to make me mer - ry ___ I will not be your

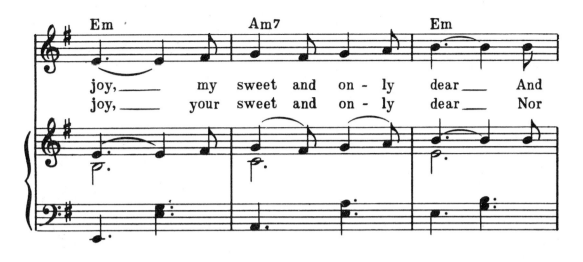

joy,_____ my sweet and on - ly dear___ And
joy,_____ your sweet and on - ly dear___ Nor

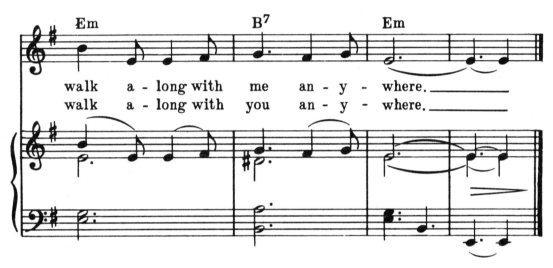

walk a - long with me an - y - where._____
walk a - long with you an - y - where._____

3. Oh madam, I would give to you a bright-red silken gown
   With nine yards a-trailing and a-drooping on the ground,
   If you will be my joy, my sweet and only dear
   And walk along with me anywhere.

4. Oh sir, I can't accept of you a bright-red silken gown
   With nine yards a-trailing and a-drooping on the ground.
   I will not be your joy, your sweet and only dear.
   Nor walk along with you anywhere.

5. Oh madam, I would give to you a little golden bell
   To ring for all your servants that they may serve you well,
   If you will be my joy, my sweet and only dear
   And walk along with me anywhere.

6. Oh sir, I shan't accept of you a little golden bell
   To ring for all my servants that they may serve me well.
   I will not be your joy, your sweet and only dear
   Nor walk along with you anywhere.

7. Oh madam, I would give to you the keys to my heart;
   Oh keep them forever and we will never part;
   If you will be my joy, my sweet and only dear
   And walk along with me anywhere.

8. Oh sir, I shall accept of you the keys to your heart,
   And keep them forever and never we will part.
   And I will be your joy, your sweet and only dear
   And walk along with you anywhere.

BARB'RY ALLEN

1. In Scar-let town ___ where I was born, ___ there
2. 'Twas in the mer - ry, mer-ry month of May, ___ when

was a fair maid dwell-in', _____ made
green buds they were swell-in'; _____ sweet

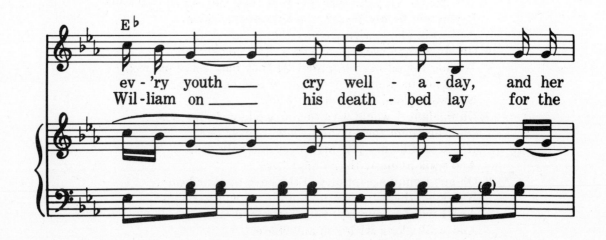

ev - 'ry youth ___ cry well - a - day, and her
Wil - liam on ___ his death - bed lay for the

name was Bar - b'ry Al - len. _____
love of Bar - b'ry Al - len. _____

3. He sent his servant to the town,
  To the place where she was a-dwellin',
  Cried, "Master bids you come to him,
  If your name be Barb'ry Allen."

    4. Then slowly, slowly she got up,
      And slowly went she nigh him,
      And when she pulled the curtains back
      Said, "Young man, I think you're dyin'."

5. "Oh, yes, I'm sick, I'm very very sick,
  And I never will be better,
  Until I have the love of one,
  The love of Barb'ry Allen."

    6. "Oh, ken ye not in yonder town
      In the place where you were a-dwellin',
      You gave a toast to the ladies all
      But you slighted Barb'ry Allen."

7. "Oh yes, I ken, I ken it well,
  In the place where I was a-dwellin';
  I give a toast to the ladies all,
  But my love to Barb'ry Allen."

    8. Then lightly tripped she down the stairs,
      He trembled like an aspen.
      'Tis vain, 'tis vain, my dear young man,
      To hone for Barb'ry Allen.

9. She walkéd out in the green, green fields.
  She heard his death bells knellin'.
  And every stroke they seemed to say,
  "Hard-hearted Barb'ry Allen."

    10. Her eyes looked east, her eyes looked west,
      She saw his pale corpse comin';
      She cried, "Bearers, bearers, put him down
      That I may look upon him."

11. The more she looked, the more she grieved,
  Until she burst out cryin';
  She cried, "Bearers, bearers, take him off,
  For I am now a-dyin'!"

    12. "Oh, father, oh, father, go dig my grave,
      Go dig it deep and narrow.
      Sweet William died for me today;
      I'll die for him tomorrow."

13. They buried her in the old churchyard,
  Sweet William's grave was nigh her,
  And from his heart grew a red, red rose,
  And from her heart a brier.

    14. They grew and they grew o'er the old church wall,
      Till they couldn't grow no higher,
      Until they tied a true lover's knot,
      The red rose and the brier.

EDWARD

Melancholy, but with motion

1. What makes that blood on the point of your knife? My
2. It is too red for your old gray mare, my
3. It is too red for your old coon dog, my

son, now tell to me.___ It is the blood of my
son, now tell to me.___ It is the blood of my
son, now tell to me.___ It is the blood of my

old_ gray mare who plowed the fields_ for
old_ coon dog who chased the fox_ for
broth - er John who hoed the corn_ for

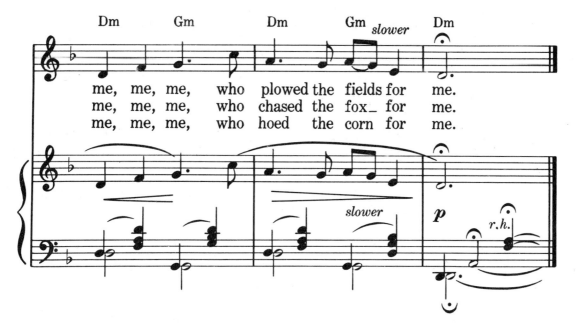

me, me, me,   who plowed the fields for me.
me, me, me,   who chased the fox_ for me.
me, me, me,   who hoed the corn for me.

4. What did you fall out about, my own dear son?
   My son, now tell to me. ·
   Because he cut yon holly bush
   Which might have been a tree, tree, tree,
   Which might have been a tree.

5. What will you say when your father comes home,
   When he comes home from town?
   I'll set my foot in yonder boat,
   And I'll sail the ocean round, round, round,
   I'll sail the ocean round.

6. When will you come back, my own dear son?
   My son, now tell to me.
   When the sun it sets in yonder sycamore tree,
   And that will never be, be, be,
   And that will never be.

I KNOW WHERE I'M GOING

3. Feather beds are soft,
   And painted rooms are bonny,
   But I would trade them all
   For my handsome, winsome Johnny.

4. Some say he's bad,
   But I say he's bonny.
   Fairest of them all
   Is my handsome, winsome Johnny.

5. I know where I'm going,
   And I know who's going with me.
   I know who I love,
   But my dear knows who I'll marry.

CROODIN DOO

3. And what did you do with the bones of the fish,
   My little wee croodin doo?
   I gave them to my wee, wee dog,
   Oh mammy, come make my bed noo.*

4. And what did your dog do when you fed him the fish,
   My little wee croodin doo?
   He laid his wee self down and died;
   Oh mammy, come make my bed noo.

   ———
   *now

THE SWAP SONG

With a happy beat - in 2

1. When I was a lit-tle boy, I lived by my-self;
   rats and the mice They led me such a life, I

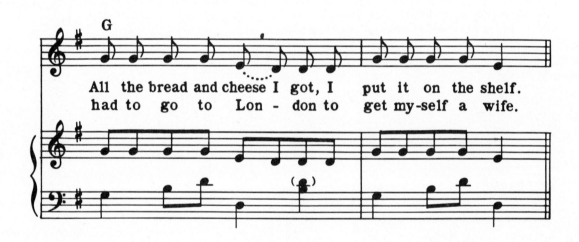

All the bread and cheese I got, I put it on the shelf.
had to go to Lon - don to get my-self a wife.

Refrain:

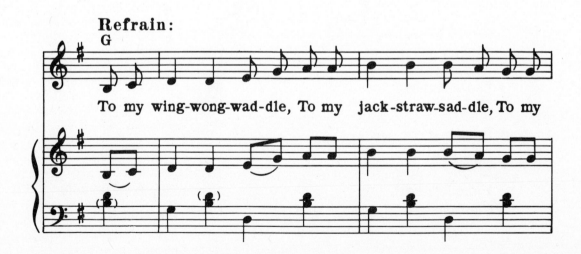

To my wing-wong-wad-dle, To my jack-straw-sad-dle, To my

john-fair-fad-dle, To my   long way   home. ___   2. The

3. The roads were so slick
   And the lanes were so narrow,
   I had to take her home
   In an old wheelbarrow.
   Chorus

4. The wheelbarrow broke
   And my wife had a fall,
   And down came wheelbarrow,
   Wife and all.
   Chorus

5. Swapped my wheelbarrow,
   Got me a horse,
   And then I rode
   From cross to cross.
   Chorus

6. Swapped my horse
   And got me a mare,
   And then I rode
   From fair to fair.
   Chorus

7. Swapped my mare
   And got me a cow,
   And in that trade
   I just learned how.
   Chorus

8. Swapped my cow
   And I got me a calf;
   In that trade
   I just lost half.
   Chorus

9. Swapped my calf
   And got me a mule,
   And then I rode
   Like a doggoned fool.
   Chorus

10. Swapped my mule
    And got me a sheep,
    And then I rode
    Myself to sleep.
    Chorus

11. Swapped my sheep
    And got me a goat;
    Rode to the 'lection,
    Sold my vote.
    Chorus

12. Swapped my goat
    And got me a rat,
    Put it in the haystack
    To run the cat.
    Chorus

13. Swapped my rat
    And I got me a hen.
    What a pretty little thing
    I had then.
    Chorus

14. Swapped my hen
    And got me a mole,
    And the doggoned thing
    Run straight in its hole.
    Chorus

THE BESTIARY

Simple - not too fast

1. Al-li-ga-tor, Hedge-hog, Ant-eat-er, Bear.
2. Mud_ tur-tle, Whale, Glow-worm, Bat,

Rat-tle-snake, Buf-fa-lo, An-a-con-da, Hare.
Sal-a-man-der, Snail, Mal-tese_ cat.

Bull - frog,_ Wood-chuck, Wol-ver-ine,_ Goose,
Black squir-rel, Ra-coon, O - pos-sum, Wren.

Whip-poor-will,— Chip-munk, Jack - al,— Moose.
Red— squir-rel, Loon, South Guin-ea hen.

3. Polecat, dog, wild otter, rat,
   Pelican, hog, dodo, bat,
   Eagle, kangaroo, sheep, duck, widgeon,
   Conger, armadillo, beaver, seal, pigeon.

4. Reindeer, blacksnake, ibis, nightingale,
   Martin, wild drake, crocodile, quail.
   Houserat, touserat, white bear, doe,
   Chickadee, peacock, bobolink, crow.

MR. FROGGIE WENT A-COURTING

sword and a pis-tol by his side,_ mm mm. _____
he had been man-y times be-fore,_ mm mm. _____

3. "Mis-sy Mous-ey are you within, mm-mm,
   Mis-sy Mous-ey are you within?"
   "Yes kind sir, I sit and spin," mm-mm.

4. He took Missy Mouse upon his knee, mm-mm,
   Took Missy Mouse upon his knee,
   Said "Missy Mouse, will you marry me?" mm-mm.

5. "Without my Uncle Rat's consent, mm-mm,
   Without my Uncle Rat's consent,
   I wouldn't marry the Pres-I-dent," mm-mm.

6. Uncle Rat laughed and shook his fat sides, mm-mm,
   Uncle Rat laughed and shook his fat sides,
   To think his niece would be a bride, mm-mm.

7. When Uncle Rat gave his consent, mm-mm,
   When Uncle Rat gave his consent,
   The weasel wrote the publishment, mm-mm.

8. Next came in was a bumblebee, mm-mm,
   Next came in was a bumblebee,
   Danced a jig with a two-legged flea, mm-mm.

9. The owl did hoot, the birds they sang, mm-mm,
   The owl did hoot, the birds they sang,
   And through the woods the music rang, mm-mm.

10. Where will the wedding breakfast be, mm-mm,
    Where will the wedding breakfast be?
    Way down yonder in a hollow tree, mm-mm.

11. What will the wedding breakfast be, mm-mm,
    What will the wedding breakfast be?
    Two green beans and a black-eyed pea, mm-mm.

12. They all went sailing across the lake, mm-mm,
    All went sailing across the lake,
    And got swallowed up by a big, black snake, mm-mm.

13. There's bread and cheese upon the shelf, mm-mm,
    There's bread and cheese upon the shelf,
    If you want any more, you can sing it yourself, mm-mm.

THE CROCODILE SONG

Comfortable, in 2

1. Come, list ye, lands-men, all to me, to tell the truth I'm
   Ship-wrecked I was one sap-py rouse, and cast all on the
2. Oh! I had not long walked a-bout when close a-long-side the
   While steer-ing close be-side the thing, I saw it was a

bound. What hap-pened to me by
shore, so I re solved to
o-cean,— 'twas there I saw
croc-o-dile, from the end of his nose to the

go-ing to the sea, and the won - ders that I found.
take a trip the coun - try to ex - plore.
some - thing move like all the earth in mo-tion.
tip of his tail he meas-ured five hun-dred mile.

CHORUS:

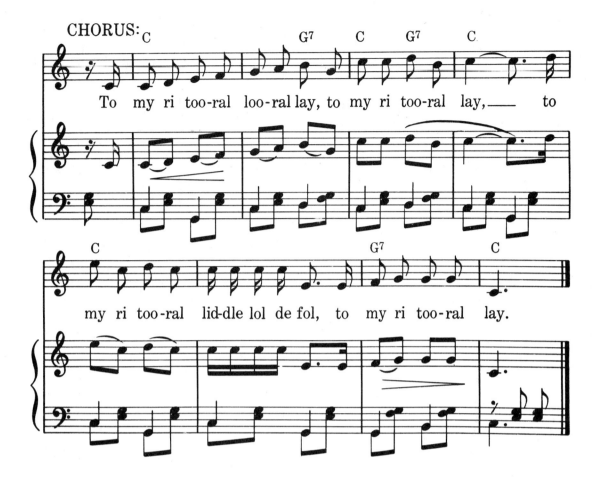

To my ri too-ral loo-ral lay, to my ri too-ral lay,—— to my ri too-ral lid-dle lol de fol, to my ri too-ral lay.

3. This crocodile, I could plainly see,
   Was none of the common race,
   For I had to climb a very tall tree
   Before I could see his face.
   Up above the wind was high,
   It blew such a hard gale from
       the south
   That I let go my hold, you see,
   And fell into the crocodile's mouth.

Chorus:
   To my ri too-ra loo-ra lay,
   To my ri too-ra lay,
   To my ri too-ra liddle lol li fol,
   To my ri too-ra lay.

4. He quickly closed his jaws on me,
   He thought to nab a victim;
   But I slipped down his throat,
       you see,
   That's the way I tricked him.

Chorus

5. I traveled on for a year or two,
   Till I got into his maw,
   And there were rum cakes not
       a few
   And a thousand pullets in store.
   Right then I banished all my cares,
   For grub I was not stinted;
   And in this crocodile I lived
       ten years,
   Right very well contented

Chorus

6. This crocodile being very old
   At last at length he died,
   He was six months in catching
       cold,
   He was so long and wide.
   His skin was ten mile thick,
       I think,
   Or very near about;
   For I was fully six months or so
   In a-digging my way out.

Chorus

PADDY AND THE WHALE

In a happy rhythm - in 2

Always G

1. Pad - dy O' Ry - an left Ire - land in glee; He
2. Pad - dy had nev - er been sail - ing be - fore, It

had a strong no - tion old Eng - land to see; He
made his heart ache when he heard the loud roar, From the

shipped in the 'Nel - lie', for Eng - land was bound, And the
glance of his eye,__ a whale he did spy, "I'm

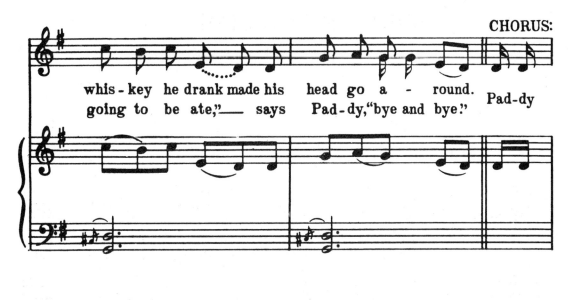

whis - key he drank made his head go a - round. Pad-dy
going to be ate,"___ says Pad-dy,"bye and bye."

whack, fol - de - rol, fol - de - rol, dol di - dee.

3. Paddy run forward, caught hold of the mast;
   He grasped his arms 'round and there he held fast.
   The boat gave a tip, and losing his grip,
   Down in the whale's belly poor Paddy did slip.
   Chorus

4. He was down in the whale six months or more,
   Till one fine day the whale he gave o'er.
   The whale gave a snort and then gave a blow,
   And out on the land poor Paddy did go.
   Chorus

5. Oh Paddy is landed and safe on the shore;
   He swears that he'll never go to sea any more.
   The next time he wishes old England to see,
   It will be when the railroad runs over the sea.
   Chorus

SONG OF THE FISHES

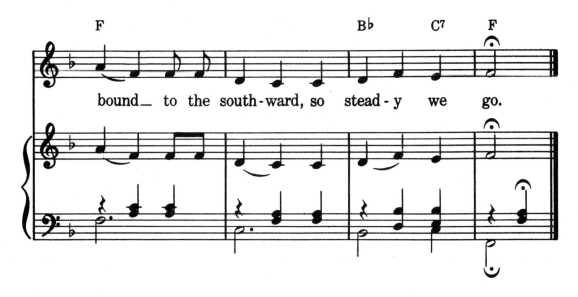

bound_ to the south-ward, so stead-y we go.

3. Next come the eels with their nimble tails,
   They jumped up aloft and loosed all the sails.

4. Next come the herrings with their little tails,
   They manned sheets and halyards and set all the sails.

5. Next comes the porpoise with his short snout,
   He jumps on the bridge and yells: "Ready, about!"

6. Next comes the swordfish, the scourge of the sea,
   The order he gives is: "Helm's a-lee!"

7. Then comes the turbot, as red as a beet,
   He shouts from the bridge: "Stick out that foresheet!"

8. Having accomplished these wonderful feats,
   The blackfish sings out next to: "Rise tacks and sheets!"

9. Next comes the whale, the largest of all,
   Singing out from the bridge: "Haul taut, mainsail, haul!"

10. Then comes the mackerel with his striped back,
    He flopped on the bridge and yelled: "Board the main tack!"

11. Next comes the sprat, the smallest of all,
    He sings out: "Haul well taut, let go and haul!"

12. Then comes the catfish with his chucklehead,
    Out in the main chains for a heave of the lead.

13. Next comes the flounder, quite fresh from the ground,
    Crying: "Damn your eyes, chucklehead, mind where you sound!"

14. Along came the dolphin, flapping his tail,
    He yelled to the boatswain to reef the foresail.

15. Along came the shark with his three rows of teeth,
    He flops on the foreyard and takes a snug reef.

16. Up jumps the fisherman, stalwart and grim,
    And with his big net he scoops them all in.

THE GOLDEN VANITY

With feeling

1. There was a ship that sailed _____ all
2. Then up stepped our cab - in boy, and

on the Low-land sea, and the name of our ship was the
bold - ly out-spoke he, and he said to our cap-tain, "What

Gold - en Van - i - ty, and we feared she would be tak-en by the
would you give to me, if I would swim a-long side of the

Span-ish en - e - my as she sailed in the Low-land,
Span-ish en - e - my, and ___ sink her in the Low-land,

Low-land, Low, as she sailed in the Low-land sea.
Low-land, Low, and sink her in the Low-land sea?"

3. "Oh, I would give you silver, and I would give you gold,
And my own fairest daughter your bonny bride shall be,
If you will swim alongside of the Spanish enemy
And sink her in the lowland, lowland, low,
And sink her in the lowland sea."

4. Then the boy he made him ready and overboard sprang he,
And he swam alongside of the Spanish enemy,
And with his brace and auger in her side he bored holes three,
And he sunk her in the lowland, lowland, low,
Yes, he sunk her in the lowland sea.

5. Then quickly he swam back to the cheering of the crew,
   But the captain would not heed him, for his promise he did rue,
   And he scorned his poor entreatings when loudly he did sue,
   And he left him in the lowland, lowland, low,
   And he left him in the lowland sea.

6. Then quickly he swam round to the port side,
   And up unto his messmates full bitterly he cried,
   "Oh, messmates, draw me up, for I'm drifting with the tide,
   And I'm sinking in the lowland, lowland, low,
   I'm sinking in the lowland sea."

7. Then his messmates drew him up, but on the deck he died,
   And they stitched him in his hammock which was so fair and wide,
   And they lowered him overboard and he drifted with the tide,
   And he sank in the lowland, lowland, low,
   And he sank in the lowland sea.

HAUL AWAY JOE

Hauntingly

1. When I was a lit-tle lad_ and so my moth-er told__
2. Lou-is was the King of France be-fore the Re-vo - lu - -
3. cook is in the gal-ley__ mak-ing duff so hand -

me,__ way, haul a-way, we'll haul a-way Joe, that
tion,__ way, haul a-way, we'll haul a-way Joe. King
y, __ way, haul a-way, we'll haul a-way Joe, and the

if I did not kiss a gal my lips would grow all
Lou-is got his head cut off which spoiled his con-sti-
cap-tain's in his ca - bin__ drink-in' wine and

HAUL AWAY JOE

mold - y. ___
tu - tion. ___ Way, haul a-way, we'll haul a-way Joe. ___
bran - dy. ___

CHORUS:

Way, haul a-way, we'll haul for bet-ter weath -

er, ___ way, haul a-way, we'll haul a-way Joe. 2. King Joe.
3. Oh, the

4. Once I had a Southern gal,
   But she was fat and lazy.
   Way, haul away, we'll haul away Joe.
   But now I've got a Yankee gal,
   And she is just a daisy.
   Way, haul away, we'll haul away Joe.
   Chorus

5. Saint Patrick was a gentleman;
   He came of dacent people.
   Way, haul away, we'll haul away Joe.
   He built a church in Dublin town
   And on it put a steeple.
   Way, haul away, we'll haul away Joe.
   Chorus

ROLLING HOME

waves we leave be-hind us seem to mur-mur as they rise: we have
sheets and crew-lines free, sir, all your bunt-lines o-ver-hauled; are the
breez-es swell to send us to our child-hood wel-come skies, to the

tar - ried here to bear you to the land you dear-ly prize.
sheer-poles and gear all read-y? Soon for New Eng-land we will steer.
glow of friend-ly fac-es and the glance of lov-ing eyes.

CHORUS:

Roll-ing home, roll-ing home, roll-ing home, a-cross the sea, roll-ing

home to dear old Eng-land, roll-ing home, dear land, to thee.

THE MAID OF AMSTERDAM

roving with you, fair maid. A - rov - ing, a -
rov - ing, since rov-ing's been my ru - i - in, I'll
go no more a rov - ing with you, fair maid.

3. Her eyes were blue, her cheeks
were brown,
Mark you well what I say,
Her eyes were blue, her cheeks
were brown,
Her hair in ringlets hanging down.

Chorus

4. I took her out and spent my pay,
Mark you well what I say,
I took her out and spent my pay,
And then this maiden just faded
away.

Chorus

BOBBY SHAFTO

bright and fair, Comb-ing down his yel-low hair,

He's my ain for ev-er-mair, Bon-nie Bob-by Shaf-to.

2. Bobby Shafto's tall and slim,
   Always dressed so neat and trim,
   Lassies they all keek* at him,
   Bonnie Bobby Shafto.
   Chorus

3. Bobby Shafto's gettin' a bairn,
   For to dangle on his airm,
   On his airm and on his knee,
   Bonnie Bobby Shafto.
   Chorus

   ———
   *to peep

73

BLOW THE WIND SOUTHERLY

Gently - in 2

CHORUS:

1. Blow the wind south-er-ly, south-er-ly, south-er-ly,
2. Blow the wind south-er-ly, south-er-ly, south-er-ly,

Blow the wind south o'er the bon-ny, blue sea.
Blow the wind south that my lov-er may come.

Blow the wind south-er-ly, south-er-ly, south-er-ly,
Blow the wind south-er-ly, south-er-ly, south-er-ly,

Blow bon - ny breeze my lov - er to me. 1. They
Blow bon - ny breeze and bring him safe home. 2. I

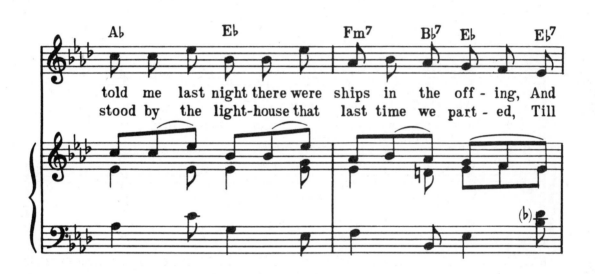

told me last night there were ships in the off - ing, And
stood by the light-house that last time we part - ed, Till

I hur - ried down to the deep, roll - ing sea; But my
dark-ness came down o'er the deep, roll - ing sea; And I

eye could not see it, wher - e'er it might be,___ The
no long-er saw the bright bark of my lov - er.

bark that is bear-ing my lov - er to me.
Blow bon - ny breeze___ and bring him to me.

3. *Chorus*

Is it not sweet to hear the breeze singing
As lightly it comes o'er the deep rolling sea?
But sweeter and dearer by far when 'tis bringing
The bark of my true love in safety to me.

WRAP ME UP IN MY
TARPAULIN JACKET

Easy-going waltz

1. Oh, had I the wings of a tur-tle-dove,
2. Oh, then let them send for two ho-ly-stones

So high on my pin-ions I'd fly.
And place them at head and at toe.

Slap! Bang! To the heart of my Pol-ly love,
Up - on them write this in - scrip-tion:

And in her dear arms I would die.
"Here lies a poor duff-er be-low."

CHORUS:

Wrap me up in my tar-pau-lin jack-et

And say a poor duff-er's laid low.

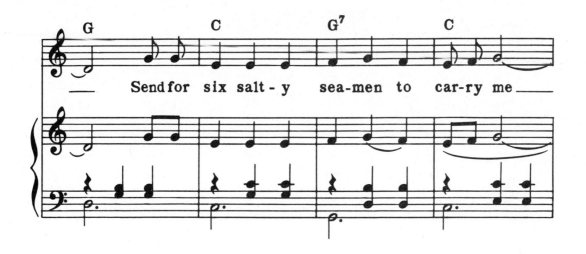

Send for six salt-y sea-men to car-ry me

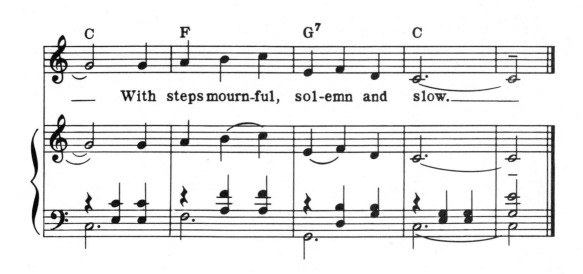

With steps mourn-ful, sol-emn and slow.

3. Then send for six jolly foretopmen,
   And let them a-rollicking go;
   And in heaping two-gallon measures
   Drink the health of the duffer below.
   Chorus

THE WHALE

Definite, in 4

1. It was in the year of forty-four, in March, the second day, that our gallant ship her anchors weighed, and for
2. And when we came to far Greenland, to Greenland cold we came, where there is frost and there is snow, and the

sea they bore — a way, brave boys, and for
might - y whale - fish-es blow, brave boys, and the

sea they bore — a - way.
might - y whale - fish - es blow.

slower

3. Our bosun went to topmast high
   With his spyglass in his hand.
   "There's a whale! There's a whale!
   There's a whalefish," he cried,
   "And she blows at every span, brave boys,
   And she blows at every span."

4. Our captain stood on the quarterdeck,
   And a brave little man was he,
   "Overhaul, overhaul, on your davit tackles fall,
   And launch your boats for sea, brave boys,
   And launch your boats for sea."

5. We struck the whale, and away we went,
   And he lashed out with his tail,
   And we lost the boat and five good men,
   And we never got that whale, brave boys,
   And we ne'er did get that darn whale.

6. Oh Greenland is an awful place
   Where the daylight's seldom seen,
   Where there is frost and there is snow,
   And the mighty whalefishes blow, brave boys,
   And the mighty whalefishes blow.

HULLABALOO BELAY

Easy-going, in 2

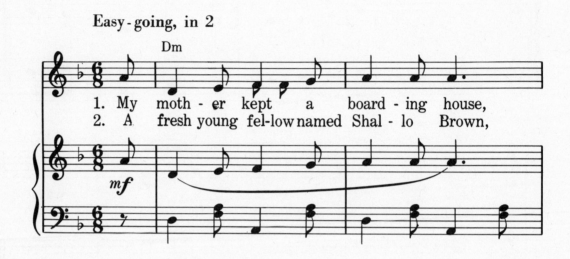

1. My moth-er kept a board-ing house,
2. A fresh young fel-low named Shal-lo Brown,

Hul-la ba-loo, be-lay; Hul-la-ba-loo, bal-
Hul-la ba-loo, be-lay; Hul-la-ba-loo, bal-

la, be-lay, and all the board-ers were
la, be-lay, fol-low'd my moth-er all

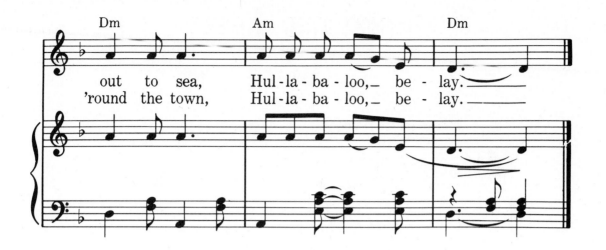

out to sea, Hul-la-ba-loo,— be-lay.
'round the town, Hul-la-ba-loo,— be-lay.

3. One day when father was on the crown
   Me mother ran off with Shallo Brown.

4. Me father says, "Young man, me b'y,"
   To which I quickly made reply,

5. Me father slowly pined away,
   Because me mother came back the next day.

RED, RED ROSES

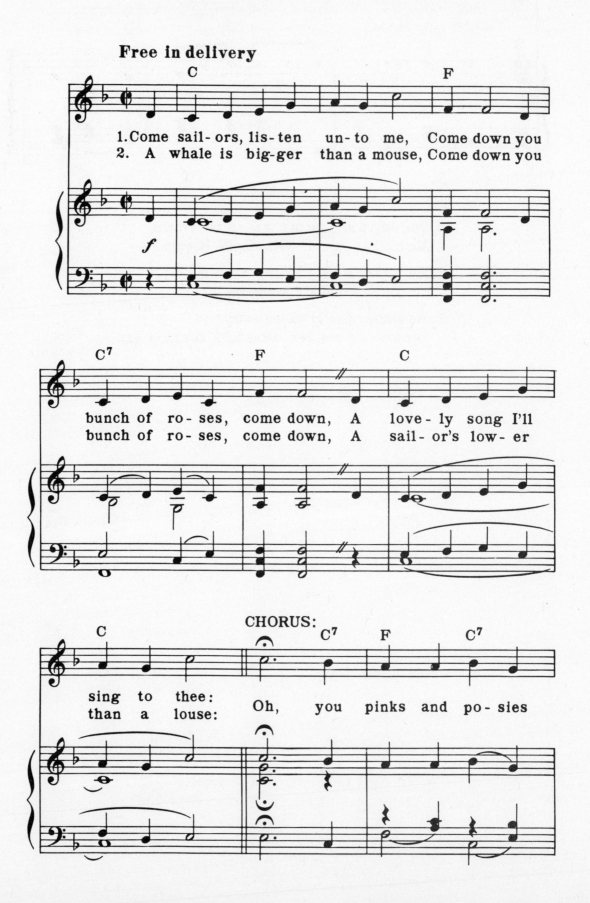

Free in delivery

1. Come sail- ors, lis- ten un- to me, Come down you bunch of ro- ses, come down, A love- ly song I'll sing to thee:
2. A whale is big- ger than a mouse, Come down you bunch of ro- ses, come down, A sail- or's low- er than a louse:

CHORUS:

Oh, you pinks and po- sies

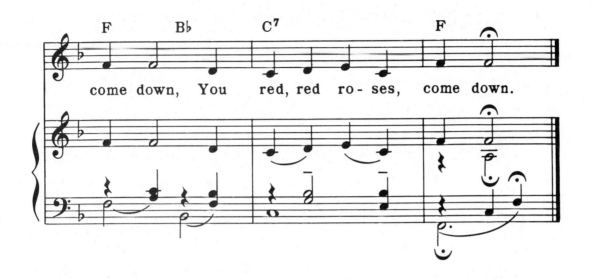

come down, You red, red ro-ses, come down.

3. The cook he rolled out all the grub,
   Come down you bunch of roses come down,
   One split pea in a ten pound tub
   Chorus

4. In eighteen hundred and fifty three,
   Come down you bunch of roses come down,
   We set sail for the Southern Sea.
   Chorus

5. In eighteen hundred and fifty five,
   Come down you bunch of roses come down,
   I was breathing but not alive.
   Chorus

6. In eighteen hundred and fifty seven,
   Come down you bunch of roses come down,
   We sailed up to the Gates of Heaven
   Chorus

7. Saint Peter would not let us in,
   Come down you bunch of roses come down,
   He sent us back to Earth again
   Chorus

8. All this is true that I do tell,
   Come down you bunch of roses come down,
   The ship we're on's a living hell
   Chorus

9. The Captain's covered o'er with fur,
   Come down you bunch of roses come down,
   Has grown a tail like a Lucifer
   Chorus

LEAVE HER, JOHNNY, LEAVE HER

Oh, the times are hard and the wag - es low,

Leave her, John - ny, leave her. I'll pack my bag and

go be-low, It's time for us to leave her. _____

2. It's growl you may but go you must, leave her, Johnny, leave her.
   It matters not if last or first, it's time for us to leave her.

3. I'm getting thin and growing sad, leave her, Johnny, leave her,
   Since first I joined this wooden-clad, it's time for us to leave her.

4. I thought I heard the first mate say, leave her, Johnny, leave her,
   "Just one more drag and then belay," it's time for us to leave her.

5. The work was hard and the voyage long, leave her, Johnny, leave her.
   The seas were high and the gales were strong, it's time for us to leave her.

6. The sails are furled, our work is done, leave her, Johnny, leave her.
   And now on shore we'll have some fun, it's time for us to leave her.

VERSION II

1. I thought I heard the old man say, leave her, Johnny, leave her,
   "You can go ashore and draw your pay," it's time for us to leave her.

2. You may make her fast and pack your gear, leave her, Johnny, leave her,
   And leave her moored to the West Street pier, it's time for us to leave her.

3. The winds were foul, the trip was long, leave her, Johnny, leave her.
   But before we go we'll sing this song, it's time for us to leave her.

4. I'll pack my bag, the ship was slow, leave her, Johnny, leave her.
   The grub was bad, the wages low, it's time for us to leave her.

5. She shipped it green and she made us curse, leave her, Johnny, leave her.
   The mate is a devil and the old man worse, it's time for us to leave her.

6. The work was hard, the voyage long, leave her, Johnny, leave her.
   The seas were high, the gales were strong, it's time for us to leave her.

7. The wind was foul and the ship was old, leave her Johnny, leave her.
   There was six feet of water in her hold, it's time for us to leave her.

8. A dollar a day is a sailor's pay, leave her, Johnny, leave her,
   To pump all night and work all day, it's time for us to leave her.

9. I'm getting thin and growing sad, leave her, Johnny, leave her,
   Since first I joined this wooden-clad, it's time for us to leave her.

10. The rats have gone, and we the crew, leave her, Johnny, leave her,
    It's time, by God, that we went too, it's time for us to leave her.

11. The sails are furled, our work is done, leave her, Johnny, leave her.
    And now on shore we'll have our fun, it's time for us to leave her.

BEN BACKSTAY

Almost like a hymn

Ben Back-stay was a bo-sun, He was a jol-ly

boy,   And none as he so mer-ri-ly could

pipe all hands a-hoy,   Could pipe all

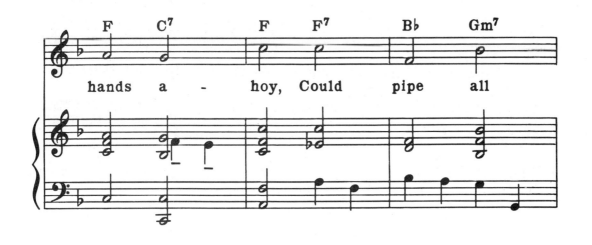

hands a - hoy, Could pipe all

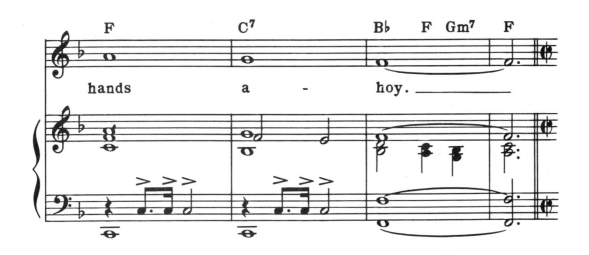

hands a - hoy. _____

CHORUS: **With a gay lilt**

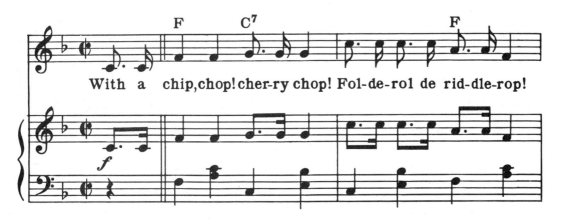

With a chip, chop! cher-ry chop! Fol-de-rol de rid-dle-rop!

Chip, chop! cher-ry chop! Fol-de-rol de ray! With a

chip, chop! cher-ry chop! Fol-de-rol de rid-dle-rop!

Chip, chop! cher-ry chop! Fol-de-rol de ray!

90

2. Once sailing with a captain who was a jolly dog,
   Our Ben and all his messmates got a double share of grog,
   A double share of grog, a double share of grog.

3. So Ben, he got tipsy, quite to his heart's content,
   And leaning o'er the starboard side right overboard he went,
   Right overboard he went, right overboard he went.
   Chorus

4. A shark was on the starboard side, and sharks no man can stand,
   For they do gobble up everything, just like the sharks on land,
   Just like the sharks on land, just like the sharks on land.

5. They threw him out some tackling to give his life some hope,
   But as the shark bit off his head he could not see the rope,
   He could not see the rope, he could not see the rope.
   Chorus

SONGS OF AMERICA GROWING

———————————————— ✦ ————————————————

The history of America in the eighteenth and nineteenth centuries is the story of a series of frontiers, each of which in turn went through several stages until it became a permanent settlement. New songs came to be written as the new country expanded. Some of these new songs were completely original; some were variations of old songs made to fit new conditions.

The immigrants passed on to their children their heritage of old-world songs, but the discipline of self and the conquest of the land created a new kind of man, and both his tribulations and his humor found reflection in new stories and song. A song subject matter grew up that reflected what was happening in the New World.

The country was alive with creative ferment and energy which found expression in singing and produced humor, beauty, anecdote, and social comment. New, or partially new, songs came out of the experiences the new country offered. There were story songs, children's songs, ballads, love songs, and play songs. Anonymous ballads, hymns, and professional songs from the entertainment field were composed and were sung everywhere. Songs were published, remembered, changed by word of mouth, and were sung for diversion in the frontier settlements. The changed anonymous versions became a part of our "folk" heritage.

Defining a folk song by use and longevity, by its quality and ability to communicate, we find that the late 18th and the 19th centuries presented us with a body of folk songs definitely American in spirit and quality. As the United States expanded from the Atlantic to the Pacific, overland and by sea, songs were created that give us insight into the attitudes and events of the American frontier as it went west, give a clear, immediate picture of the various occupations and modes of men's lives at that time—clearer and more immediate by far than what can be gleaned from histories, or even from historical novels. These are the songs out of America's growth.

In the beginning there was no entertainment except from the raconteur of tall tales, the fiddler, or the ballad singer. Songs had a unique function: there was no radio, no orchestra, no place to go. Evenings at home, housewarmings, camp meetings, barn dances, travelers meeting for a night meant self-entertainment.

After the Revolutionary War, singing groups, minstrel shows, vaudeville shows created songs that became a part of America's musical life. Many of these exhibited in content or melody a lasting value. They became as much a part of the folk song of America as did the anonymous ballads from Europe and the songs of local poets.

From the 1830's on, the vaudeville stage expanded rapidly, featuring comic songs on every sort of subject. Concert artists began to travel the country and popularized their songs. A considerable number of families traveled together as troupes. Two of the most famous were the Hutchinson and the Baker families. Their family programs included solos, ensembles, and both vocal and instrumental pieces. The most famous and best-remembered songs, however, came from the minstrel shows that became so popular after 1832.

Professional American song writers began to flourish in the cities. There was Samuel Woodworth, Henry Clay Work, George Root, Stephen Foster, and others. Their music was published as sheet music and widely sung on the variety and concert stages. You could hear their songs on the clipper ships and in frontier cabins. You would hear other songs like "Joe Bowers," parodies of these popular composers.

Whether listening or singing, the people found songs staples of entertainment. They were written in every possible form and still in the old tradition. Tin Pan Alley had not yet taken over and standardized a "pop" form. Songs had to express emotion, tell a story, convey humor or drama or lyric mood. That is why the songs of those days reflect important moments in the American legend and spirit, in a way that latter-day songs seldom do.

The stories in song covered events of every kind; gave a canvas of characters that form a mosaic of American profiles. The subject matter or the point of view could be male or female, good or bad, serious or amusing. The way of life led to a uniquely American play of fancy, turn of wit, hush of lullaby, or antic of human and animal.

THE INDIAN CHRISTMAS CAROL

Like a march, not too fast

Play left hand like a bass drum, but softly.

1. 'Twas in the moon of win-ter-time when all the birds had fled, that might-y Gitch-i-man-i-tou sent an-gel choirs in-stead. Be-fore their light the stars grew dim and

2. With-in a lodge of bro-ken bark the ten-der Babe was found, a rag-ged robe of rab-bit skin en-wrapped His beau-ty round. The chiefs from far be-fore Him knelt with

3. O chil-dren of the for-est free, o sons of Man-i-tou, the Ho-ly Child of earth and heav'n is born to-day for you. Come kneel be-fore the ra-diant boy who

won-d'ring hunt-ers heard the hymn:
gifts of fox and bea-ver pelt: Je-sus, your king, is born,
brings you beau-ty peace and joy.

Je - sus is born in ex - cel-sis glo - ri - a.

ON SPRINGFIELD MOUNTAIN

nay hoo - i too di noo.

2. He scarce had mowed half round the field
   When an ug-lye serpent bit his heel.

   Chorus:

3. They took him home to Mol-lye dear
   Which made her feel so ve-rye queer.

   Chorus:

4. Now Mol-lye had two ruby lips
   With which the pizen she did sip.

   Chorus:

5. Now Mol-lye had a rotten tooth
   And so the pizen killed them both.

THE DREADNOUGHT

Steady

1. There's a sau-cy wild pack-et, and a pack-et of fame; she be-longs to New York, and The Dread-nought's her name; she is bound to the

2. The time of her sail-ing is_ now draw-ing nigh; fare - well, pret-ty May, I must bid you good - bye; fare - well to old

3. Oh, the Dreadnought is pulling out of Waterlock dock
Where the boys and the girls to the pierheads do flock.
They will give us three cheers while their tears do flow,
Saying, "God bless the Dreadnought where'er she may go!"

4. Oh, the Dreadnought's a-bowlin' down the wild Irish sea
Where the passengers are merry, their hearts full of glee,
While her sailors like lions walk the decks to and fro.
She's the Liverpool packet, oh Lord, let her go!

98

west-ward where the storm-y winds blow; bound a-
Eng-land and all there we hold dear, bound a-

way in the Dread-nought, to the west-'ard we'll go.
way in the Dread-nought, to the west-'ard we'll steer.

5. Oh, the Dreadnought's a-sailin' the Atlantic so wide,
While the dark, heavy seas roll along her black sides,
With her sails neatly spread and the Red Cross to show.
She's the Liverpool packet, oh Lord, let her go!

6. Oh the Dreadnought's becalmed on the banks of Newfoundland
Where the water's so green and the bottom is sand,
Where the fish of the ocean swim round to and fro.
She's the Liverpool packet, oh Lord, let her go!

7. Oh, the Dreadnought, she's a-bowlin' past old Nantucket Head,
And the man in the chains takes a cast with the lead;
Then up jumps the flounders just fresh from the ground,
Crying, "Blast your eyes, Chucklehead; and mind where you sound!"

8. Oh the Dreadnought's arrived in America once more;
We'll go ashore, shipmates, on the land we adore,
See our wives and our sweethearts, be merry and free,
Drink a health to the Dreadnought, wheresoe'er she may be.

9. Here's a health to the Dreadnought, and to all her brave crew;
Here's a health to her captain and officers, too.
Talk about your flash packets, *Swallow Tail* and *Black Ball*,
But the Dreadnought's the clipper to beat one and all.

BLOW THE MAN DOWN

give me some time to blow the man down.
give me some time to blow the man down.

3. 'Twas on a Black Baller I first served my time,
   And on that Black Baller I wasted my prime.

4. 'Tis when a Black Baller's preparing for sea
   You'd split your sides laughing at sights that you see.

5. With the tinkers and tailors and soljers and all
   That ship for prime seamen on board a Black Ball.

6. 'Tis when a Black Baller is clear of the land,
   Our Boatswain then gives us the word of command.

7. "Lay aft," is the cry, "to the break of the Poop!
   Or I'll help you along with the toe of my boot!"

8. 'Tis larboard and starboard on the deck you will sprawl,
   For "Kicking Jack" Williams commands the Black Ball.

9. Pay attention to orders, now you one and all,
   For right there above you flies the Black Ball.

STORMALONG

Very slow – almost free in delivery

3. We'll lower him down with a golden chain,
   To my way, hay, ay, Stormalong;
   Our eyes are dim but not with rain,
   To my way, hay, ay, Mister Stormalong.

4. A good, old skipper to his crew,
   To my way, hay, ay, Stormalong;
   An able sailor, brave and true,
   To my way, hay, ay, Mister Stormalong.

5. He's moored at last and furled his sail,
   To my way, hay, ay, Stormalong;
   All free from wrecks and far from gales,
   To my way, hay, ay, Mister Stormalong.

6. Old Stormy, he's heard the bugle call,
   To my way, hay, ay, Stormalong;
   Now sing his dirge, please, one and all,
   To my way, hay, ay, Mister Stormalong.

THE SAILOR'S GRAVE

like the twi-light dawn ____ of an au-tumn day. ____
He ___ smiled and died ____ in his mess-mate's arms. __

3. We had no costly winding sheet;
   We placed two round shot at his feet,
   And in his hammock snug and sound,
   A kingly shroud, like marble bound.

4. We proudly decked his funeral vest
   With the starry flag upon his breast;
   We gave him this as a badge so brave;
   Then he was fit for a sailor's grave.

5. Our voices broke, our hearts turned weak,
   And tears were seen on the brownest cheek;
   A quiver played on the lip of pride
   As we lowered him down our ship's dark side.

6. A splash, a plunge, and our task was o'er,
   And the billows rolled as they rolled before,
   And many a prayer said to the wave
   That lowered him in a sailor's grave.

SKIP TO MY LOU

skip to my Lou, my dar' wup! She's gone a-gain, skip — to my Lou, she's gone a-gain, skip — to my Lou, she's gone a-gain, skip — to my Lou, skip to my Lou, my dar-ling.

3. I've lost my girl, now what'll I do?
4. I'll get another one prettier than you.
5. Chicken on the haystack, shoo, shoo, shoo.
6. Pa's got a shotgun, Number 32.
7. Hurry up, slowpoke, do, oh do.
8. My girl wears a number nine shoe.
9. When I go courting, I take two.
10. He's got big feet and awkward too.
11. Kitten in the haymow, mew, mew, mew.
12. I'll get her back in spite of you.
13. We'll keep it up till half past two.
14. One old boot and a run-down shoe.
15. Stole my partner, skip to my Lou.

POOR LITTLE TURTLE DOVE

With feeling (free in delivery)

Poor lit-tle tur-tle dove, set-ting on a pine,

Long-ing for his own true love as I did once for

mine, for mine, as I did once for mine.

2. I come down the mountainside
   I give my horn a blow
   Everywhere them pretty girls
   Said yonder goes my beau, my beau,
   Yonder goes my beau.

3. I went down in the valley green
   To win to me my love,
   When I done with that pretty little girl
   She turned to a turtle dove, a dove,
   She turned to a turtle dove.

4. I walked down the street that very same night,
   On my heart was a sweet, sweet song
   Got in a fight and in jail all night
   And every durn thing went wrong, went wrong,
   Every durn thing went wrong.

5. I went up on the mountainside
   And I took a swig of corn,
   Possum wrapped his tail around a blackberry bush
   Two mountain lions were born, were born,
   Two mountain lions were born.

6. Poor little turtle dove,
   Setting on a pine,
   Longing for his own true love
   As I once did for mine, for mine,
   As I once did for mine.

OLD JOE CLARK

CHORUS:

Fare thee well, old__ Joe Clark, Fare thee well, I say.

Fare thee well, old__ Joe Clark, Hear my gui-tar play.

3. Sixteen horses in my team,
   The leaders they are blind;
   Every time the sun goes down,
   Got a pretty gal on my mind.
   Chorus

4. Wish I had a nickel,
   Wish I had a dime,
   Wish I had a pretty li'l gal
   For to kiss her an' call her mine.
   Chorus

5. I went up on the mountain top
   To give my horn a blow.
   I thought I heard my sweetheart say,
   "Yonder comes my beau."
   Chorus

6. Eighteen miles of mountain road
   And fifteen miles of sand.
   If I ever travel this road again
   I'll be a married man.
   Chorus

7. Old Joe Clark's a mean old man,
   I'll tell you the reason why:
   He tore down my old rail fence
   So his cattle could eat my rye.
   Chorus

8. I went down to old Joe Clark's,
   I did not mean no harm;
   He grabbed his old forty-four
   And shot me through the arm.
   Chorus

9. I went down to old Joe Clark's,
I found old Joe in bed;
I stuck my finger in old Joe's eye
And killed old Joe stone dead.
Chorus

10. Yonder sits a turtle dove,
Sitting on yonder pine;
You may weep for your true love
And I shall weep for mine.
Chorus

11. Wouldn't marry his widow,
Tell you the reason why:
Her neck's so long and stringy, boys,
Afraid she would never die.
Chorus

12. Wish I was in Arkansas
Sitting on a rail,
Jug of whiskey under my arm
And a 'possum by the tail.
Chorus

13. Wish I had a sweetheart;
I'd set her on a shelf;
And every time she smiled at me
I'd get up there myself.
Chorus

VERSION II

The jaybird and the sparrowhawk,
They fly all round together,
Had a fight in the briar patch
And never lost a feather.
Chorus

The jaybird in the sugar tree,
The sparrow on the ground;
The jaybird shaked the sugar down,
The sparrow passed it round.
Chorus

The jaybird died with the whooping
cough,
The sparrow with the colic.
Along came a terrapin with a fiddle
on his back.
Inquiring the way to the frolic.
Chorus

Old Joe Clark had a cow,
She was muley born;
It takes a jaybird a week and a half
To fly from horn to horn.
Chorus

Old Joe Clark had a yellow cat,
She would neither sing or pray;
She stuck her head in the buttermilk
jar
And washed her sins away.
Chorus

Old Joe Clark had a dog
As blind as he could be,
Ran a redbug around a stump
And a coon up a holler tree.
Chorus

LEATHER-WINGED BAT

Brightly - in 2

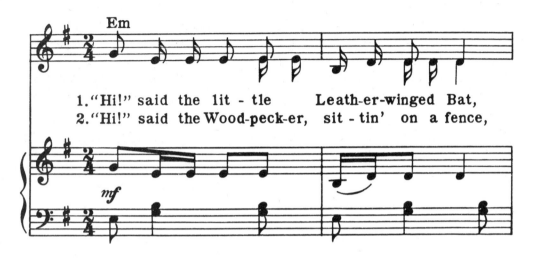

1. "Hi!" said the lit - tle Leath-er-winged Bat,
2. "Hi!" said the Wood-peck-er, sit - tin' on a fence,

"I'll tell you ___ the rea - son that, The
"Once I court - ed a hand - some wench.

rea - son that I fly in the night is be-
She got sau - cy and from me fled;

LEATHER-WINGED BAT

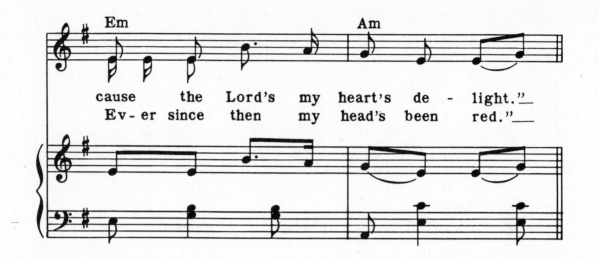

cause   the   Lord's   my   heart's   de - light."__
Ev - er since   then   my   head's   been   red."__

CHORUS:

How - dee, Dow - dee   did - dle - o - day;

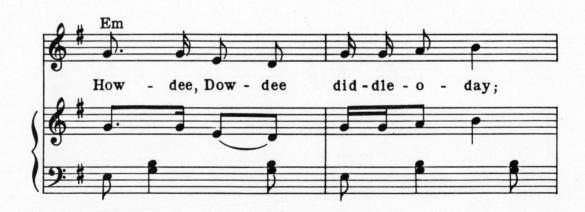

How - dee, Dow - dee   did - dle - o - day;

How - dee, Dow - dee did - dle - o - day;

Ho - lo - lee - dee did - dl - ee doe.___

3. "Hi," said the bluebird as she flew,
   "If I were a young man, I'd have two.
   If one got saucy and wanted to go,
   I'd have a new string to my bow."

Chorus:
Howdee, dowdee, diddle-o-day,
Howdee, dowdee, diddle-o-day,
Howdee, dowdee, diddle-o-day,
Hololee-dee diddlee doe.

MY OLD 'COON DOG

Waltz with a lilt

My old coon dog, my old coon dog, I

wish you'd bring him back. _____ He

chased the old sow o-ver the fence, And the

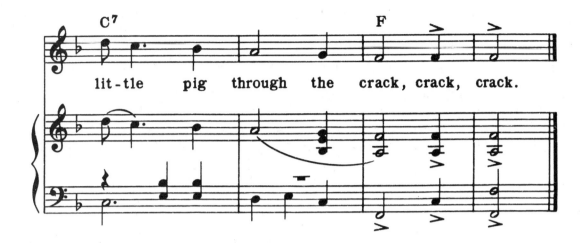

lit - tle   pig   through   the   crack, crack, crack.

2. My old 'coon dog, my old 'coon dog,
   He chased a 'coon up a tree,
   And when I shot that racoon down,
   It was twice as big as me.

3. My old 'coon dog, my old 'coon dog,
   He went to chase a 'coon;
   He started the chase at the first of March
   And ended the tenth of June.

4. My old 'coon dog, my old 'coon dog,
   He died one afternoon;
   I woke with a fright that very same night
   And heard him chasing a 'coon.

5. My old 'coon dog, my old 'coon dog,
   I wish you'd bring him back;
   He chased the old sow over the fence
   And the little pig through the crack, crack, crack.

OLD BLUE

In 2, but not too fast

1. I had an old dog _____ and his name was
2. Chased that 'pos-sum _____ up a 'sim-mon

Blue, _____ and I bet-cha five
tree; _____ Blue looked at the

dol-lars he's a good dog too, ___ say-in', "Come on,
'pos-sum, 'pos-sum looked at me ___ say-in', "Go on,

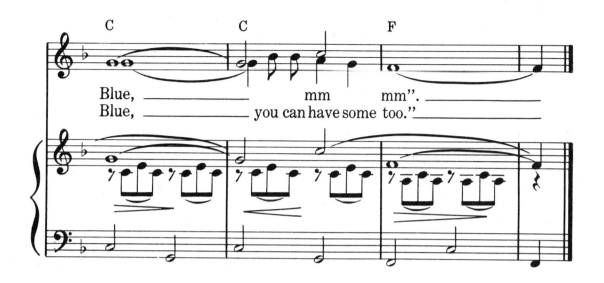

Blue, _____ mm mm". _____
Blue, _____ you can have some too."

3. Baked that 'pos-sum, good and brown,
   Laid them sweet potatoes 'round and 'round,
   Saying, "Come on, Blue,
   You can have some too."

4. Old Blue died and he died so hard,
   That he jarred the ground in my backyard,
   Saying, "Go on, Blue,
   I'm a-comin' too."

5. I dug his grave with a silver spade,
   And I let him down with a golden chain,
   Saying, "Go on, Blue,
   I'm a-comin' too."

6. When I get to Heaven, first thing I'll do,
   Grab my horn, and I'll blow for OLD BLUE,
   Saying, "Come on, Blue,
   Fin'lly got here too."

GROUND HOG

Whis-tle up yer dog and load yer gun,—

Whis-tle up yer dog and load yer gun.— We're

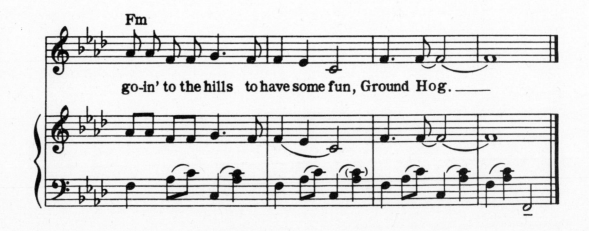

go-in' to the hills to have some fun, Ground Hog.—

2. Big old fellow, a-sittin' on a log, (repeat)
   I heard him whistle and I knowed he was a hog, ground hog.

3. Big old fellow, as big as a bear, (repeat)
   The meat we'll eat, the hide we'll wear, ground hog.

4. Get away, Sam, gonna load my gun, (repeat)
   The ground hog hunt has just begun, ground hog.

5. Come here, John, with your great big pole, (repeat)
   And twist this ground hog out of his hole, ground hog.

6. Here he is, boys, the hole's wore slick, (repeat)
   Come on, Sam, with your fork'ed stick, ground hog.

7. Up jumped Sam with a ten-foot pole, (repeat)
   He jabbed it into that ground hog's hole, ground hog.

8. Work, boys, work for all you earn, (repeat)
   Skin him after dark and tan him in a churn, ground hog.

9. Out he comes and begins to whirl, (repeat)
   He's the biggest ole ground hog in the world, ground hog.

10. Sam cocked his gun and John pulled the trigger, (repeat)
    But the fellow that got him was old Joe Digger, ground hog.

11. Up stepped Sal with a snigger and a grin, (repeat)
    "Whatcha goin' to do with the ground hog skin?" Ground hog.

12. The children screamed and the children cried, (repeat)
    They love that ground hog cooked and fried, ground hog.

13. Dragged him home and put him in to boil, (repeat)
    I knowed he was a ground hog, I could smell him for a mile, ground hog.

14. Hello, mama, make John quit, (repeat)
    He's eatin' all the hog and I can't get a bit, ground hog.

15. Hello, boys, oh ain't it a sin, (repeat)
    Watch that gravy run down Sam's chin! Ground hog.

16. Old Aunt Sally come a-skipping down the hall, (repeat)
    We got enough whistle pig to feed 'em all. Whistle pig.

LET'S GO A-HUNTING

Happy waltz

1. "Let's go a-hunt-in'," says Risk-y Rob, —
2. "What shall I hunt?" says Risk-y Rob, —

"Let's go a-hunt-in'," says Rob-in to Bob;
"What shall I hunt?" says Rob-in to Bob;

"Let's go a-hunt-in'," says Dan-'l and Joe,
"What shall we hunt for?" says Dan-'l and Joe,

"Let's go a - hunt-in'," says Bil-ly Bar-low.
"Hunt for a rat," cried Bil-ly Bar-low.

3. "How shall we take him?" says Risky Rob.
   "How shall we take him?" says Robin to Bob.
   "How shall we take him?" says Dan'l and Joe.
   "Go borry a gun," cried Billy Barlow.

4. "How shall we haul him?" says Risky Rob.
   "How shall we haul him?" says Robin to Bob.
   "How shall we haul him?" says Dan'l and Joe.
   "Go borry a cart," says Billy Barlow.

5. "How shall we divide him?" says Risky Rob.
   "How shall we divide him?" says Robin to Bob.
   "How shall we divide him?" says Dan'l and Joe.
   "How shall we divide him?" says Billy Barlow.

6. "I'll take the shoulder," says Risky Rob.
   "I'll take the side," said Robin to Bob.
   "I'll take the ham," said Dan'l and Joe.
   "Tail bone mine," cried Billy Barlow.

7. "How shall we cook him?" says Risky Rob.
   "How shall we cook him?" says Robin to Bob.
   "How shall we cook him?" says Dan'l and Joe.
   "How shall we cook him?" cried Billy Barlow.

8. "I'll broil the shoulder," says Risky Rob.
   "I'll fry the side," says Robin to Bob.
   "I'll boil the ham," says Dan'l to Joe.
   "Tail bone raw," cried Billy Barlow.

MISTER RABBIT

With a gay bounce - in 2

1. Mis-ter Rab-bit, Mis-ter Rab-bit,   Your
2. Mis-ter Rab-bit, Mis-ter Rab-bit,   Your

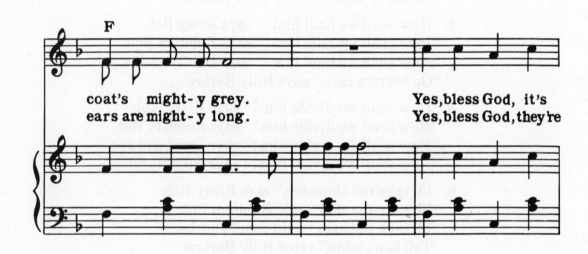

coat's might-y grey.   Yes, bless God, it's
ears are might-y long.   Yes, bless God, they're

made that way.—   Ev-'ry lit-tle soul must shine,   shine,
put on wrong.

Ev-'ry lit-tle soul must shine,   shine. _____

3. Mister Rabbit, Mister Rabbit, your ears are mighty thin.
   Yes, bless God, they're splitting the wind.
   Chorus

4. Mister Rabbit, Mister Rabbit, your eyes are mighty red.
   Yes, bless God, I'm almost dead.
   Chorus

THE GREY GOOSE

Rather fast in 2

1. Last Sun-day morn-ing, Lord, Lord, Lord,
2. dad-dy went a-hunt-ing, Lord, Lord, Lord, oh, my

last Sun-day morn-ing, Lord, Lord, Lord. 2. Oh, my
dad-dy went a-hunt-ing, Lord, Lord, Lord.

3. He went hunting for the grey goose.
   He went hunting for the grey goose.

4. And he took along his shot-gun,
   Yes, he took along his shot-gun.

5. And along come a grey goose,
   Yes, along come a grey goose.

6. Well it's up to his shoulder,
   And he pulled back the hammer.

7. And the gun went a-booloo,
   Oh, the gun went a-booloo.

8. He was six weeks a-fallin',
   He was six weeks a-fallin'.

9. And they had a feather-pickin',
   Oh, your wife and my wife.

10. He was nine months a-cookin',
    He was nine months a-cookin'.

11. Then they put him on the table,
    Yes, they put him on the table.

12. And the knife couldn't cut him,
    No, the knife couldn't cut him.

13. And the fork couldn't stick him,
    No, the fork couldn't stick him.

14. And the saw couldn't cut him,
    He broke the saw's tooth out.

15. So they took him to the hogpen,
    And the hogs wouldn't eat him.

16. And the last time I see'd him,
    Oh, the last time I see'd him.

17. He was flying o'er the ocean
    He was flying o'er the ocean

18. With a long string of goslins,
    With a long string of goslins.

19. They was all going "Quink, quank,"
    They was all going "Quink, quank."

20. That's the story of the grey goose,
    That's the story of the grey goose.

CARELESS LOVE

Not too slow, in 2

1. Love, oh, love, oh, care-less love.____ I
(2.) love my mam-my and my pap-py, too.____ I

Love, oh, love, oh, care-less love.____ I
love my mam-my and my pap-py, too.____ I

Love, oh, love, oh, care-less love, can't you
love my mam-my and my pap-py, too; gon-na

see, what love has done to me?_____ 2. I
leave 'em both and go with you._____

3. It's on this railroad bank I stand,
   On this railroad bank I stand,
   It's on this railroad bank I stand;
   I know I'm gonna kill a railroad man.

   Chorus

DARLIN' CORY

Like "The Blues" - free in delivery

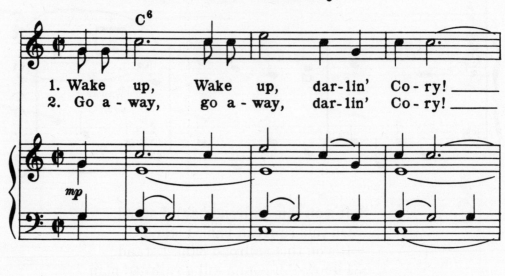

1. Wake up, Wake up, dar-lin' Co-ry!
2. Go a-way, go a-way, dar-lin' Co-ry!

What makes you sleep so sound?
Stop hang-in' 'round my bed.

The rev-e-nue
Bad lik-ker's

3. I'm a-goin' across the deep ocean,
I'm a-goin' across the deep sea,
I'm a-goin' across the deep ocean,
Just to bring darlin' Cory to me.

4. Go dig me a hole in the meadow,
Go dig me a hole in the ground,
Go dig me a hole in the meadow,
Just to lay darlin' Cory down.

5. Don't you hear them bluebirds a-singing?
Don't you hear that mournful sound?
They're a-preaching Cory's funeral
In some lonesome graveyard ground.

6. Wake up, wake up, darlin' Cory!
What makes you sleep so sound?
The revenue officers a-comin',
Gonna tear your still house down.

SWEET KITTY KLOVER

Waltz – but rather free in delivery

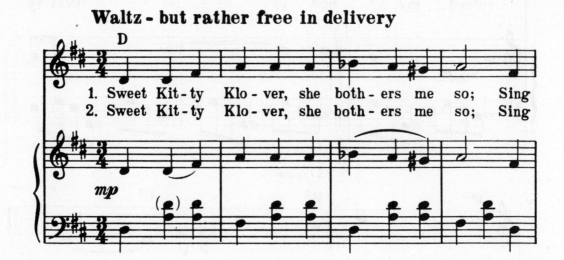

1. Sweet Kit-ty Klo-ver, she both-ers me so; Sing
2. Sweet Kit-ty Klo-ver, she both-ers me so; Sing

wack - fid - dle - dee, Sing wack - fid - dle - doe. Where
wack - fid - dle - dee, Sing wack - fid - dle - doe. If

sweet Kit-ty lives I am bound__ to go, Sing
Kit - ty to church with me__ would go, Sing

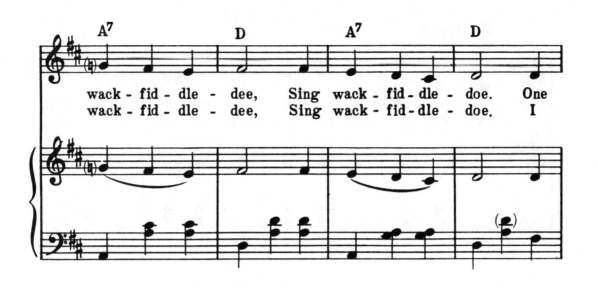

wack - fid - dle - dee,   Sing wack - fid - dle - doe.   One
wack - fid - dle - dee,   Sing wack - fid - dle - doe.   I

moon - lit night,   ah me   what bliss, Through a
think I should nev-er be wretch-ed a - gain   If

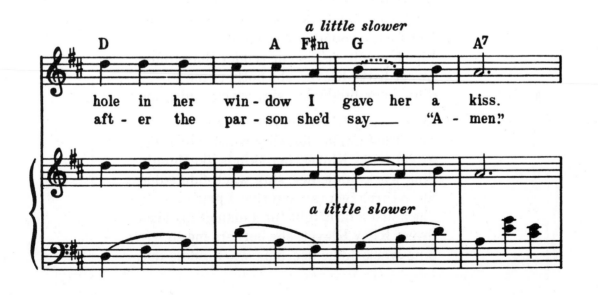

hole in her win - dow I gave her a kiss.
aft - er the par - son she'd say___ "A - men."

a little slower

Tempo I

Sweet Kit - ty Klo - ver she both - ers me so; Sing
Sweet Kit - ty Klo - ver she both - ers me so; Sing

wack - fid - dle - dee, Sing wack - fid - dle - doe.
wack - fid - dle - dee, Sing wack - fid - dle - doe.

3. Sweet Kitty Klover, she bothers me so,
   Sing wack-fiddle-dee, sing wack-fiddle-doe.
   Sweet Kitty Klover, she bothers me so,
   Sing wack-fiddle-dee, sing wack-fiddle-doe.
   Her face is round and red and fat
   Like a pulpit cushion or redder than that.
   Sweet Kitty Klover, she bothers me so,
   Sing wack-fiddle-dee, sing wack-fiddle-doe.

4. Sweet Kitty Klover in person is low,
   Sing wack-fiddle-dee, sing wack-fiddle-doe.
   Sweet Kitty Klover, her skin is like dough,
   Sing wack-fiddle-dee, sing wack-fiddle-doe.
   She's three feet tall and that I prize;
   She's just a fit height for a man of my size.
   Sweet Kitty Klover, she bothers me so,
   Sing wack-fiddle-dee, sing wack-fiddle-doe.

JENNIE JENKINS

JENNIE JENKINS

CHORUS:

Gon - na buy me a ring, Fol - de -
ray, Fol - de - rol - dy - tol - dy - day. _____
Roll, _____ Jen - nie Jen - kins, roll. _____

3. Will you wear red, my dear, O dear?
   Oh, will you wear red, Jennie Jenkins?
   No, I won't wear red,
   It's the color of my head.
   Chorus

4. Will you wear black, my dear, O dear?
   Oh, will you wear black, Jennie Jenkins?
   No, I won't wear black,
   It's the color of my back.
   Chorus

5. Will you wear purple, my dear, O dear?
   Oh, will you wear purple, Jennie Jenkins?
   No, I won't wear purple,
   It's the color of a turkle.
   Chorus

6. Will you wear green, my dear, O dear?
   Oh, will you wear green, Jennie Jenkins?
   No, I won't wear green,
   For it's a shame to be seen.
   Chorus

DOWN IN THE VALLEY

hear   the   wind   blow. _____
hear   the   wind   blow. _____

3. Roses love sunshine,
   Violets love dew,
   Angels in heaven
   Know I love you.

4. If you don't love me,
   Love who you please,
   Put your arms 'round me,
   Give my heart ease.

5. Give my heart ease, love,
   Give my heart ease,
   Put your arms 'round me,
   Give my heart ease.

6. Write me a letter,
   Send it by mail,
   Send it in care of
   The Birmingham Jail.

7. Birmingham Jail,
   Birmingham Jail,
   Send it in care of
   The Birmingham Jail.

8. Build me a castle
   Forty feet high,
   So I can see her
   As she rides by.

9. As she rides by, love,
   As she rides by,
   So I can see her,
   As she rides by.

10. Down in the valley,
    The valley so low,
    Hang your head over,
    Hear the wind blow.

LOLLY TOO-DUM DAY

Steady, in 2

1. As I went out one morn-in' to take the pleas-ant air, Lol-ly-too-dum, too-dum, lol-ly-too-dum-day; as I went out one
2. You bet-ter go wash them dish-es and hush that flat-ter-in' tongue, Lol-ly-too-dum, too-dum, lol-ly-too-dum-day; you bet-ter go wash them
3. "O pit-y my con-di-tion, just like you would your own," Lol-ly-too-dum, too-dum, lol-ly-too-dum-day; "O pit-y my con-

morn - in' to take the pleas - ant air, I
dish - es and hush that flat-ter - in' tongue, for you
di - tion, just like you would your own: for

o - ver - heard a moth-er a - scold-in' her daugh-ter
know that you want to git mar-ried, and that you are too
four - teen long years I've been liv - in' a -

fair, Lol-ly - too - dum, too - dum, lol-ly - too-dum-day. —
young, Lol-ly - too - dum, too - dum, lol-ly - too-dum-day. —
lone," Lol-ly - too - dum, too - dum, lol-ly - too-dum-day. —

4. "Supposin' I were willin', where would you git your man?" *(repeat)*
"Lawdy massy, Mammy, I'd marry that handsome Sam."

5. "Supposin' he should spite you like you done him before?" *(repeat)*
"Lawdy massy, Mammy, I could marry forty more!

6. "They's peddlers and they's tinkers and boys from the plow; *(repeat)*
Lawdy massy, Mammy, I'm a-gittin' that feeling now!"

7. "Now my daughter's married and well-fer-to-do, *(repeat)*
Gather round, young fellers, I'm on the market, too!"

141

SOURWOOD MOUNTAIN

Steady, like a square dance

1. Chick - en a - crow-ing on Sour - wood Moun-tain,
2. My true love is a blue - eyed dai - sy,
3. My true love lives at the head of the hol - ler,
4. Ducks in the pond, geese in the o - cean,

hoe dee-ing_ di did-dy-I - day;

So man-y pret-ty girls,
If I don't get_ her
She won't come and
Dev-il's in wom - an

I can't count 'em,
I'll go cra - zy,
I won't fol - ler,
if she takes the no-tion,

hoe dee-ing di did-dy-I - day.

COTTON-EYE JOE

Free in delivery

1. Where do you come from? Where do you go?
(2.) come fer to see you, Come fer to sing,

Where do you come from,___ Cot-ton-Eye Joe? 2.Well, I
Come fer to show you my dia - mond ring.

143

GO WAY FROM MY WINDOW

Gentle - without rhythm

1. Go a - way from my win - dow, _____ Go a -
2. I gave back her pres - ents, _____ She

way_ from my door. _____ Go a -
gave_ back the ring, _____ But I'll

way, way, way from my bed - side And both - er me no
al - ways love my_ dar - ling As long as song birds

more,____ And both-er me no more.
sing,____ As long as song birds sing.

3. Please go and tell my brothers,
   Tell all my sisters too,
   That the reason that my heart is broke
   Is all because of you,
   Is all because of you.

4. Go away from my window,
   Go away from my door,
   Go away, way, way from my bedside
   And bother me no more,
   And bother me no more.

MISSOURI MULE

Slow - Free in delivery

Old Mis-sou-ri had a mule; He-haw, he-haw, he-haw.

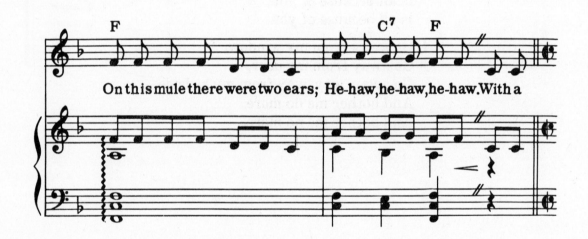

On this mule there were two ears; He-haw, he-haw, he-haw. With a

Happy - in 2

flip-flop here, and a flip-flop there. Here a flop, there a flop,

ev-'ry-where a flip-flop. Old Mis-sou-ri

had a mule; He-haw, he-haw, he-haw.

2. Old Missouri had a mule, he-haw, he-haw, he-haw.
   On this mule there was a tail, he-haw, he-haw, he-haw.
   *With a swish-swish here, and a swish-swish there,
   Here a swish, there a swish and everywhere a swish-swish,
   With a flip-flop here, and flip-flop there,
   Here a flop, there a flop and everywhere a flip-flop,
   Old Missouri had a mule, he-haw, he-haw, he-haw.

3. Old Missouri had a mule, he-haw, he-haw, he-haw.
   And on this mule there were two heels, he-haw, he-haw, he-haw.
   With a kick-kick here, and a kick-kick there,
   Here a kick, there a kick and everywhere a kick-kick,
   With a swish here and a swish there,
   Here a swish, there a swish and everywhere a swish-swish,
   With a flip-flop here, and a flip-flop there,
   Here a flop, there a flop and everywhere a flip-flop,
   Old Missouri had a mule, he-haw, he-haw, he-haw.

*In cumulative songs, always add the lines from previous verse to new verse.

HUSH LITTLE BABY

Pa- pa's gon- na buy you a dia - mond ring.
Pa- pa's gon- na buy you a bil - ly goat.

3. If your billy goat don't pull,
   Papa's gonna buy you a cart and bull.
   If that cart and bull turn over,
   Papa's gonna buy you a dog named Rover.

4. If your dog named Rover don't bark,
   Papa's gonna buy you a horse and cart.
   If that horse and cart fall down,
   You'll be the sweetest little baby in town.

OH, YOU NEW YORK GIRLS

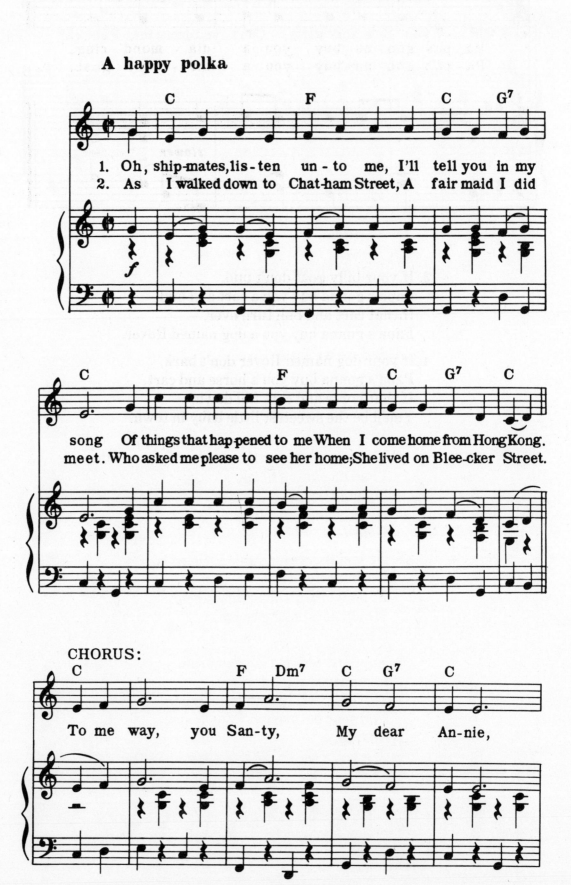

A happy polka

1. Oh, ship-mates, lis-ten un-to me, I'll tell you in my song Of things that hap-pened to me When I come home from HongKong.

2. As I walked down to Chat-ham Street, A fair maid I did meet. Who asked me please to see her home; She lived on Blee-cker Street.

CHORUS:

To me way, you San-ty, My dear An-nie,

Oh, you New York girls, Can't you dance the Pol-ka?

3. "Now if you'll only come with me,
   You can have a treat,
   You can have a glass of brandy,
   And something nice to eat."
   Chorus

4. Before we sat down to eat
   We had several drinks,
   The liquor was so awful strong,
   I quickly fell asleep.
   Chorus

5. When I awoke next morning,
   I had an aching head,
   My gold watch and my pocketbook
   And the lady friend had fled.
   Chorus

6. On looking around this little room,
   Nothing could I see
   But a woman's shoes and apron
   Which now belong to me.
   Chorus

7. Now dressed in a lady's apron,
   I wandered most forlorn,
   Till Martin Churchill took me in
   And sent me around Cape Horn.
   Chorus

151

THE PIRATE SONG

Waltz

1. My boat's by the tow-er, and my bark's on the bay, and
2. For-give my rough mood un-ac-cus-tomed to sue; I

both must be gone at the dawn of the day. The
woo not, per-haps, as your land-lub-bers do. My

moon's in her shroud, and to light thee a-far on the
voice is at-tuned to the sound of the gun that

deck of the dar-ing's a love-light-ed star. So,
star-tles the deep when the com-bat's be-gun.

CHORUS:

wake, la-dy, wake, I am wait-ing for thee, oh, this night or

nev-er my bride thou shalt be, so, bride thou shalt be.

3. The Frenchman and Don will flee
  from our path,
And the Englishman cower below
  at our wrath,
And our sails shall be gilt
  in the gold of the day,
And the sea robins sing as we
  roll on our way.

   Chorus

4. A hundred shall serve—the best
  of the brave—
And the chief of a thousand
  shall kneel as thy slave,
And thou shalt reign queen,
  and thy empire shall last
Till the black flag by inches
  is torn from the mast.

   Chorus

153

TURKEY IN THE STRAW
(ZIP COON)

In a gay dance tempo

1. As__ I was go-in'__ down the road, a__ tired team an' a heav-y load, I__crack'd my whip and the lead-er sprung and says,__ day-day, to the wag-on tongue.

2. Oh,__ I went out to milk, and I did-n't know how; I__ milked a goat in-stead of a cow. A__ mon-key sit-tin' on a pile of straw, a-wink-in' his eye at his moth-er-in-law.

CHORUS:

Tur - key in the straw, tur - key in the hay;
Tur - key in the hay, tur - key in the straw, the

dance_ all _ night and work _ all _ day;
old _ gray _ mare won't gee _ nor _ haw;

Roll 'em up and twist 'em up a - high, tuck - a - haw, and_

hit 'em up a tune_ call'd_ Tur - key in the Straw.

155

3. Well, I met Mister Catfish comin' down the stream;
   Says Mister Catfish, "What does you mean?"
   I caught Mister Catfish by the snout,
   And turned Mister Catfish wrong side out.

4. Then I come to the river and I couldn't get across,
   So I paid five dollars for an old blind hoss.
   Well, he wouldn't go ahead and he wouldn't stand still,
   So he went up and down like an old sawmill.

5. As I came down the new-cut road,
   I met Mister Bullfrog, I met Miss Toad,
   And every time Miss Toad would sing,
   The old Bullfrog cut a pigeon wing.

BUCKEYE JIM

With a gay lilt

1. Way up yon-der a-bove the sky   A blue-bird lived in a
2. Way up yon-der a-bove the moon;   A blue-jay nest in a

CHORUS:

jay-bird's eye.
sil-ver moon.   Buck-eye Jim   you can't go! __ Go

weave and spin, you can't go, __   Buck-eye Jim. __

3. Way down yonder in a woodland trough
   An old woman died of the whooping cough. *Chorus*

4. Way down yonder in a hollow log
   A red bird danced with a green bullfrog. *Chorus*

ALL DAY ON THE PRAIRIE
(THE COWBOY)

Waltz - steady rhythm

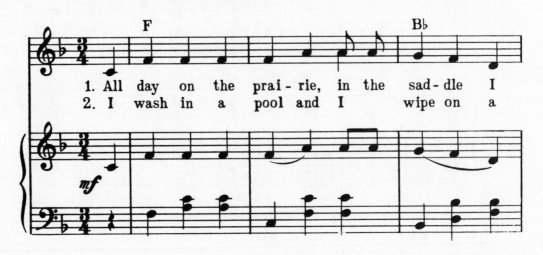

1. All day on the prai - rie, in the sad - dle I
2. I wash in a pool and I wipe on a

ride; Not e - ven a dog, boys, to trot by my
sack; I car - ry my ward - robe__ all on my

side; My fire I must kin - dle with chips gath - ered
back; For want of an ov - en I cook bread in a

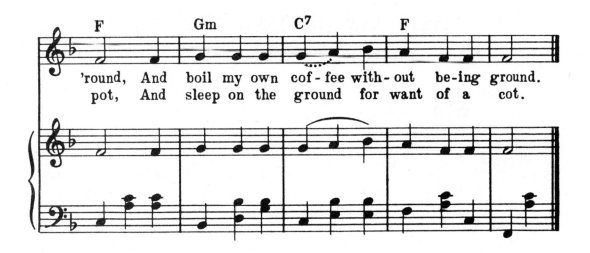

'round, And boil my own cof-fee with-out be-ing ground.
pot, And sleep on the ground for want of a cot.

3. My ceiling is the sky, my floor is the grass,
   My music is the lowing of the herds as they pass,
   My books are the brooks, my sermons the stones,
   My parson is a wolf on his pulpit of bones.

4. My books teach me ever consistence to prize;
   My sermons, that small things I should not despise;
   My parson remarks from his pulpit of bones,
   And Luck favors those who look out for their own.

5. O Cupid's a friend to the rich, not the bold,
   And the best of his arrows are pointed with gold.
   With me romance always ends with grief,
   Because of the salary I make punchin' beef.

6. I have hair on my chin, I could pass for the goat
   That bore all the sins in the ages remote;
   Society bans me, so savage and dodge,*
   That the Masons would blackball me out of their lodge.

   ————————
   *evasive and shifty

THE YOUNG MAN WHO
WOULDN'T HOE CORN

Free in delivery

1. I'll sing you a song, and it's not ver-y long, a-
2. He went to the field, and he took a peep in: the

bout a young man who would-n't hoe corn. The
weeds and the grass was up to his chin, the

fast (in 2)

rea - son why, I can't tell, for
weeds and the grass, they were so high, they

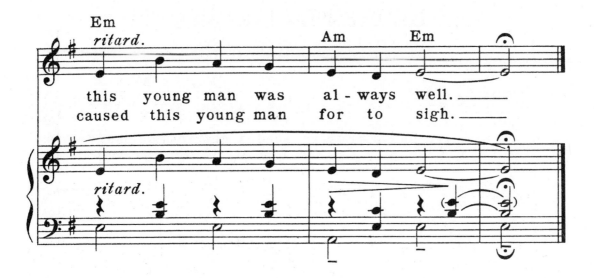

this young man was al-ways well. _____
caused this young man for to sigh. _____

3. He went down to his neighbor's door
   Where he had been many times before;
   Pretty little miss, will you marry me,
   Pretty little miss, what do you say?

4. Well, here you air a-wantin' for to wed
   And cannot make your own corn bread.
   Single I be, single I remain;
   A lazy man I won't maintain.

5. Now go down to that cute little widder,
   And I hope that you don't git her.
   She gave him the mitten as sure as you're born,
   Because this young man wouldn't hoe corn.

THE LITTLE OLD SOD SHANTY
(THE WESTERN SETTLER)

Steady, in 2

1. I'm look-ing rath-er seed-y now while hold-ing down my
2. I rath-er like the nov-el-ty of liv-ing in this

claim; my vit-tles are not al-ways of the best,___ and the
way, though my bill of fare is-n't al-ways of the best,___ but I'm

mice play shy-ly round me as I nes-tle down to rest in my
hap-py as a clam on the land of Un-cle Sam in my

lit-tle old_ sod shan-ty on the plain.___
lit-tle old_ sod shan-ty in the west.___ Oh, the

CHORUS:

hing-es are of leath-er and the win-dows have no glass,   the
boards,they let the howl-ing bliz-zard in._____   You can
see the hun-gry coy-ote, as he sneaks up through the grass to my
lit-tle old_ sod shan-ty on the   claim.____

3. Oh, when I left my eastern home a bachelor so gay
To try to win my way to wealth and fame,
Oh, I little thought I'd come down to burning twisted hay
In my little old sod shanty on my claim. *Chorus*

4. Still I wish some kind-hearted girl would pity on me take
And relieve me from this mess that I am in.
Oh the angel, how I'd bless her if this her home she'd make,
The little old sod shanty on my claim. *Chorus*

163

GREER COUNTY BACHELOR

Waltz

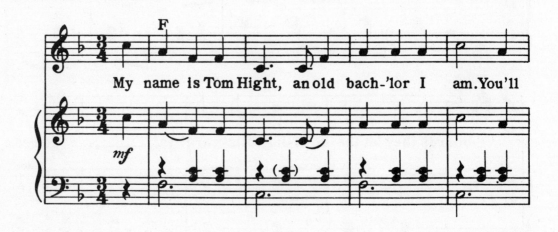

My name is Tom Hight, an old bach-'lor I am. You'll

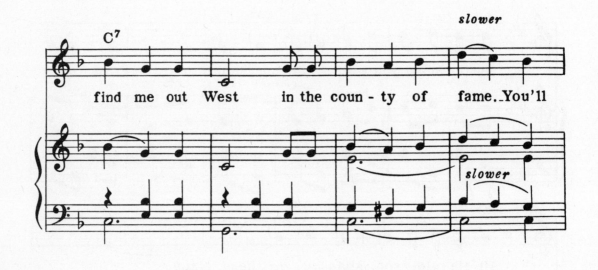

find me out West in the coun-ty of fame. You'll

find me out West on an el-e-gant plain,

Starv-ing to death on my gov-ern-ment claim.

2. Hurrah for Greer County! The land of the free,
   The land of the bedbug, grasshopper, and flea;
   I'll sing of its praises, I'll tell of its fame,
   While starving to death on my government claim.

3. How happy am I when I crawl into bed;
   A rattlesnake hisses a tune at my head,
   A gay little centipede, all without fear,
   Crawls over my pillow and into my ear.

4. My clothes is all ragged as my language is rough,
   My bread is corn-dodgers, both solid and tough;
   But yet I am happy, and live at my ease
   On sorghum molasses and bacon and cheese.

5. Good-by to Greer County where blizzards arise,
   Where the sun never sinks and a flea never dies,
   And the wind never ceases but always remains
   Till it starves us to death on our government claims.

6. Farewell to Greer County, farewell to the West,
   I'll travel back east to the girl I love best;
   I'll travel back to Texas and marry me a wife,
   And quit eating corn-dodgers for the rest of my life.

DREARY BLACK HILLS

A waltz - but rather free in delivery

bills; Each day they keep start-ing for the drear-y Black Hills.
Bill Will lift up your hair___ on the drear-y Black Hills.

3. I got to Cheyenne, no gold did I find;
   I thought of the lunch route I left far behind.
   Through wind, sand and storm, wet plumb to the gills;
   They call me the orphan of the dreary Black Hills.

4. Don't go away, stay at home if you can,
   Stay away from that city, they call it Cheyenne,
   Where the blue waters roll and Comanche Bill
   Will lift up your hair on the dreary Black Hills.

167

PATRICK ON THE RAILROAD

Easygoing, in 2

1. In eigh - teen hun - dred and for - ty-one, I
2. In eigh - teen hun - dred and for - ty-two, I

put my cor - d'roy breech - es on, put my cor - d'roy
left the ould world for the new, bad 'cess to the luck that

breech - es on to work up - on the rail - way.
brought me through to work up - on the rail - way.

CHORUS:

Billy me-oo, re-eye, re-aye, Billy me-oo, re-eye, re-aye, Billy me-oo, re-eye, re-aye, to work upon the railway.

3. When we left Ireland to come here
And spend our latter days in cheer,
Our bosses, they did drink strong
    beer,
And we worked on the railway.
Chorus

4. Our contractor's name it was Tom
    King.
He kept a store to rob the men,
A Yankee clerk with ink and pen
To cheat Pat on the railway.
Chorus

5. It's "Pat, do this," and "Pat,
    do that!"
Without a stocking or a hat,
And nothing but an old cravat,
While Pat works on the railway.
Chorus

6. One Monday morning to our
    surprise,
Just half an hour before sunrise,
The dirty divil went to the skies,
And Pat worked on the railway.
Chorus

DRILL YE TARRIERS

With a lilt - in 2

Ev - 'ry morn - ing at sev - en o' - clock There's a

hun - dred tar - ri - ers a - work - ing at the rock. The

boss comes a - long and he says, "Keep still!

Come down heav - y on the cast i - ron drill and

170

CHORUS:

drill, ye tar-ri-ers, drill. Drill, ye tar-ri-ers, drill. O, it's work all day for sug-ar in your tay,

Down be-hind the rail-way. Drill, ye tar-ri-ers, drill, And blast, And fire."

DRILL YE TARRIERS

2. Now our foreman was Gene McCann,
   By God, he was a blame mean man.
   Last week a premature blast went off
   And a mile in the air went big Jim Goff.
   Chorus

3. The next time payday come around,
   Jim Goff a dollar short was found.
   When asked what for, came this reply,
   "You were docked for the time you were up in the sky."
   Chorus

4. The boss was a fine man down to the ground
   And he married a lady six feet round.
   She baked good bread and she baked it well,
   But she baked it hard as the holes of hell.
   Chorus

off
172

THE DYING HOGGER

Slow like a dirge - in 3

1. A hog-ger on his death-bed lay; His
2. A mar-ble slab I do not crave; Just

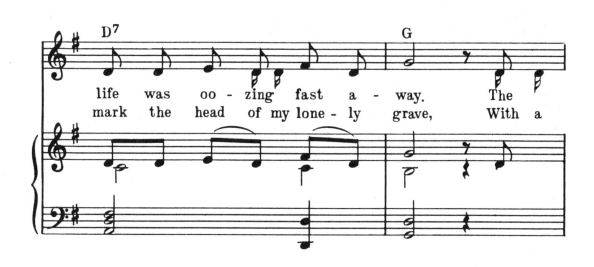

life was oo-zing fast a-way. The
mark the head of my lone-ly grave, With a

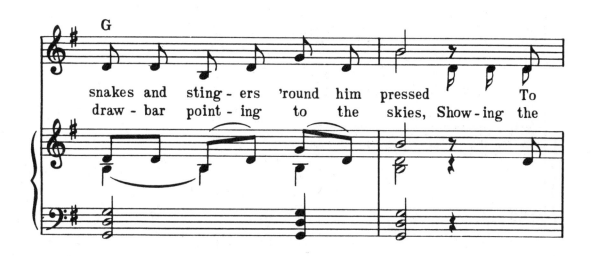

snakes and sting-ers 'round him pressed To
draw-bar point-ing to the skies, Show-ing the

THE DYING HOGGER

fore I soar be-yond the stars. ___ Just
see him crawl from un-der a wreck ___ With a

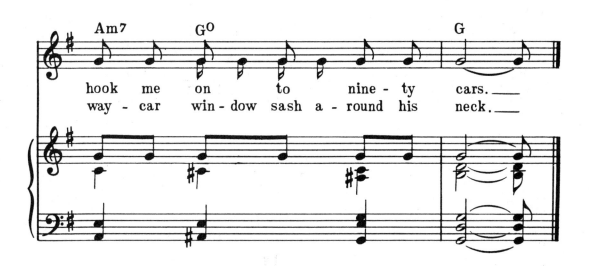

hook me on to nine-ty cars. ___
way-car win-dow sash a-round his neck. ___

3. "And you, dear friends, I'll have to thank,
If you'll let me die at the water tank,
Within my ears that old-time sound:
A tallow-pot pulling the tank-spout down.
And when at last in the grave I'm laid,
Let it be in the cool of the water tank shade.
And put within my cold, still hand
A monkey-wrench and the old oil can."

JOE BOWERS

Lively, but free in delivery

1. My name it is Joe Bow-ers, and I've got a broth-er
2. I used to court a gal there; her name was Sal-lie

Ike; I'm just here from old Mis - sou - ri, and
Black; I asked her if she'd mar - ry me, she

all the way from Pike; I tell you why I
said it was a whack; says she to me, "Joe

left there   and   why   I   be-gan   to   roam,   and
Bow - ers,   be - fore we're hitched   for   life,   you

left   my   ag-ed   par-ents,   so   far   a-way from home.
ought   to get a   lit-tle home to   keep your lit-tle   wife."

3. Says I, "My dearest Sally,
   O Sally, for your sake,
   I'll go to California
   And try to raise a stake."
   Says she to me, "Joe Bowers,
   You are the one to win."
   She gave me a kiss to seal
     the bargain—
   And I throwed a dozen in.

4. I'll never forget my feelings
   When I bid adieu to all.
   Sal, she cotched me round the neck
   And I began to bawl.
   When I began they all commenced,
   You never heard the like,
   How they all took on and cried
     and cried
   The day I left old Pike.

5. When I got to this country,
   I had nary a red,
   I had such wolfish feelings,
   That I wished myself most dead.
   But the thoughts of my dear Sally
   Soon made this feeling git:
   And whispered hopes to Bowers,
   Lord I wish I had 'em yit.

6. At last I went to mining,
   Put in my biggest licks,
   Come down upon the boulders
   Just like a thousand bricks.
   I worked both late and early
   In rain and sun and snow,
   I was working for my Sally,
   It was all the same to Joe.

177

SIOUX INDIANS

Free in delivery

1. I'll sing you a song, though it may be a sad one, of
2. I crossed the Mis-sour-i and joined a large train which

trials_ and trou-bles, and where first be - gun. I
bore us o'er moun-tain and val - ley and plain; and

left my dear kin-dred, my friends, and my home, and we
of-ten of eve-nings out hunt - ing we'd go to

178

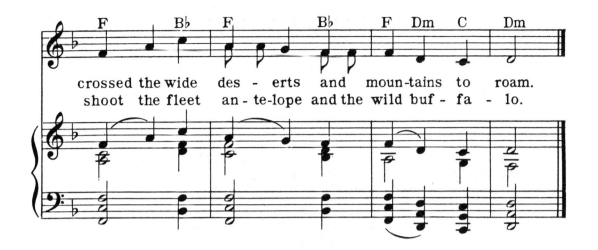

crossed the wide des - erts and moun-tains to roam.
shoot the fleet an - te-lope and the wild buf - fa - lo.

3. Without any money provisions to buy
   We'd sneak 'round the hills shooting elk on the sly;
   We'd shoot the fat deer and take him to town
   To buy flour to bake bread, and tea, a few pound.

   4. We heard of Sioux Indians, all out on the plains
      A-killin' poor drivers and burning their trains—
      A-killin' poor drivers with arrows and bow,
      When captured by Indians no mercy they'd show.

5. We traveled three weeks till we came to the Platte,
   And pitched out our tents at the head of a flat;
   We'd spread down our blankets on the green grassy ground,
   While our horses and oxen were a-grazing around.

   6. While taking refreshments we heard a low yell,
      The whoop of Sioux Indians coming up from the dell;
      We sprang to our rifles with a flash in each eye.
      "Boys," says our brave leader, "we'll fight till we die."

7. We gathered our horses, got ready to fight,
   As the band of Sioux Indians just came into sight.
   They came down upon us with a whoop and a yell,
   At the crack of our rifles oh six of them fell.

   8. They made a bold dash and came near to our train,
      And the arrows fell down just like hail and like rain,
      But with our long rifles we fed them cold lead
      'Til many a brave warrior around us lay dead.

9. With our small band, there were just twenty-four,
   And of the Sioux Indians there were five hundred or more,
   We fought them with courage, we spoke not a word,
   'Til the end of the battle that was all that was heard.

   10. We shot their bold Chief at the head of the band,
       He died like a warrior with the gun in his hand,
       When they saw their full Chief laying dead in his gore,
       They whooped and they yelled and we saw them no more.

11. We hitched up our horses and started our train,
    Three more bloody battles this trip on the plain.
    And in our last battle three of our brave boys they did fall,
    And we left them to rest in a green shady dell.

    12. We traveled by day, guarded camp during night,
        Till Oregon's mountains look'd high in their might
        Now at Pocahontas beside a clear stream
        Our journey has ended in the land of our dream.

THE HAND CART SONG

Like a hymn (in 2)

1. Ye saints who dwell on Eu-rope's shore, pre-
Chorus: For some must push and some must pull as
2. For you must cross the rag-ing main be-

pare your-selves for man-y more,— to leave be-hind your
we go march-ing up— the hill, so mer - ri - ly on our
fore the prom-ised land— you gain, and with the faith - ful

na - tive land, for sure, God's judg-ments are at hand.
way we go, un - til we reach the val - ley, oh!
make a start to cross the plains with your hand -cart.

180

3. The lands that boast of
    modern light,
We know are all as dark as night,
Where poor men toil and want
    for bread,
Where peasant hosts are blindly led.

4. These lands that boast of liberty,
You ne'er again would wish to see,
When you from Europe make a start
To cross the plains with
    your hand cart.

Chorus

5. As on the road the carts are pulled,
'Twould very much surprise
    the world,
To see the old and feeble dame
Thus lend a hand to pull the same.

6. And maidens fair will dance
    and sing,
Young men as happy as a king.
And children too will laugh and play,
Their strength increasing day
    by day.

Chorus

7. But some will say it is too bad
The saints upon the foot to pad.
And more than that to pull a load,
As they go marching o'er the road.

8. But then we say it is the plan,
To gather up the best of men,
And women too, for none but they
Will ever travel in this way.

Chorus

9. And long before the valley's
    gained,
We will be met upon the plains,
With music sweet and friends
    so dear,
And fresh supplies our hearts
    to cheer.

10. And then with music and with
    song,
How cheerfully we'll march along,
And thank the day we made a start
To cross the plains with
    our hand cart.

Chorus

11. When you get there among
    the rest,
Obedient be and you'll be blest,
And in God's chambers be shut in
With judgments cleanse the
    earth from sin.

12. For we do know it will be so,
God's servants spoke it long ago,
We say it is high time to start
To cross the plains with
    our hand cart.

Chorus

THE UTAH IRON HORSE

I - ron Horse is com-ing with a train in his wake.
see those dread-ful dives,_ how they lynch man - y lives.

3. If alive we shall be,
   Many folks we shall see,
   Nobles, lords, flotsam, beggars,
   Among us will come the slavers.
   Saints will come, sinners too.
   We'll have all that we can do,
   For this great Union Railroad
   It will fetch the devil through.

A RIPPING TRIP
(*Air*—"POP GOES THE WEASEL")

1. You go aboard of a leaky boat,
And sail for San Francisco;
You've got to pump to keep
   her afloat,
You have *that*, by jingo.
The engine soon begins to squeak,
But nary thing to oil her;
Impossible to stop the leak—
   Rip goes the boiler!

2. The captain on the promenade,
Looking very savage;
Steward and the cabin maid
Fighting 'bout a cabbage;
All about the cabin floor,
Passengers lie seasick;
Steamer's bound to go ashore,
   Rip goes the physic!

3. "Pork and beans" they
   can't afford
To second cabin passengers;
The cook has tumbled overboard
With forty pounds of sassengers!
The engineer, a little tight,
Bragging on the Mail line,
Finally gets into a fight,
   Rip goes the engine!

4. The cholera begins to rage,
A few have got the scurvy;
Chickens dying in their cage,
Steerage topsy-turvy.
When you get to Panama,
Greasers want a back-load;
Officers begin to jaw,
   Rip goes the railroad!

5. When home, you'll tell an
   awful tale,
And always will be thinking
How long you had to pump and bail,
To keep the tub from sinking.
Of course you'll take a glass of gin,
'Twill make you feel so funny;
Some city sharp will rope you in,
   Rip goes your money!

ACRES OF CLAMS

(*Air*—"ROSIN THE BOW")

Like a waltz

1. No long-er the slave of am - bi - tion,____
2. For each man who got rich by min - ing,____

— I laugh at the world and its shams,
— Per - ceiv - ing that hun-dreds grew poor,

As I think of my pleas-ant con - di - tion,
I made up my mind to try farm-ing,

hap-py con-di-tion,__ Sur-round-ed by a-cres of clams.__

3. So rolling my grub in my blanket,
   I left all my tools on the ground;
   I started one morning to shank it
   For the country they call Puget Sound.
   Chorus

4. Arriving flat broke in midwinter,
   I found it enveloped in fog
   And covered all over with timber
   Thick as hair on the back of a dog.
   Chorus

5. When I looked on the prospects so gloomy,
   The tears trickled over my face,
   And I thought that my travels had brought me
   To the end of the jumping-off place.
   Chorus

6. I staked me a claim in the forest
   And sat myself down to hard toil;
   For two years I chopped and I worked it,
   But I never got down to the soil.
   Chorus

7. I tried to get out of the country,
   But poverty forced me to stay
   Until I became an old settler;
   Then nothing could drive me away.
   Chorus

8. No longer the slave of ambition,
   I laugh at the world and its shams,
   As I think of my pleasant condition
   Surrounded by acres of clams.
   Chorus

THE BLUE TAIL FLY

Free in delivery

1. When I was young I used to wait on my
2. And when he'd ride in the af-ter-noon, I'd
3. One day he ride a-round the farm; the

mas-ter and give him his plate, and
fol-low af-ter with a hick-o-ry broom; the
flies so nu-mer-ous they did swarm; one

pass the bot-tle when he got dry, and brush a-way the
po-ny be-ing rath-er shy when bit-ten by a
chanc'd to bite him in the thigh; the dev-il take the

CHORUS:

blue-tail fly. Jim-mie crack corn and I don't care,

Jim-mie crack corn and I don't care, Jim-mie crack corn and

I don't care, my mas-ter's gone a - way.

4. The pony run, he jump, he pitch,
He threw my master in the ditch.
He died, and the jury wondered why—
The verdict was the blue-tail fly. *Chorus*

5. They lay him under a 'simmon tree;
His epitaph is there to see:
"Beneath this stone I'm forced to lie,
A victim of the blue-tail fly." *Chorus*

COME YOURSELVES AND SEE
(*Air*—"BLUE TAIL FLY")

1. There is no land upon the earth
   Contains the same amount of worth,
   And he that could not here reside
   Had ought to freeze the other side!

   Chorus: You who don't believe it
   You who don't believe it
   You who don't believe it,
   Come yourselves and see!

2. We've got more gold than all the world,
   A flag that wins whene'er unfurled
   And smarter men to help us through
   Than England, France, or Mexico.   *Chorus*

3. We've smarter ships than Johnny Bull,
   Larger sheep with finer wool;
   A prison too you cannot fail
   To throw a bull through by the tail.   *Chorus*

4. We raise the largest cabbage heads,
   Got more and better feather beds.
   Of everything we've got the best
   And thieves until you cannot rest.   *Chorus*

5. All ruffianism now is o'er,
   The country's safer than before;
   Our cities keep the rowdies straight
   Or wend them through the golden gate.   *Chorus*

6. We've got the highest mountains here,
   Taller trees and faster deer,
   And travel more, at higher rates,
   Than people in the eastern states.   *Chorus*

7. We've got the smartest river boats
   And, ten to one, old whiskey bloats;
   We're blest with very heavy fogs
   And any amount of poodle dogs!   *Chorus*

8. We've got a few unmarried G'hals,
   Railroads, ditches, and canals;
   Although we did repudiate,
   A joke 'twas only to create.   *Chorus*

9. To one and all, both young and old,
   You're welcome to the land of gold;
   So come along, be not afraid,
   We guarantee you all well paid!   *Chorus*

THE SHADY OLD CAMP
(*Air*—"BEN BOLT")

Free in delivery

1. Oh, don't you re-mem-ber the shad-y old camp, That
2. Oh, don't you re-mem-ber the cool, sum-mer breeze, So

stood by the side of the brook, Where we lay on the ground aft-er
wel-come in June and Ju - ly, __ And the ta- ble that stood 'neath the

man-y a tramp, And the fire-place where we __ used to
shad-y oak trees, At the foot of the moun-tain so

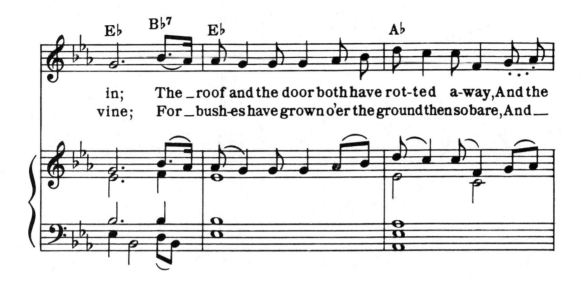

in;   The _ roof and the door both have rot-ted a-way, And the
vine;   For _ bush-es have grown o'er the ground then so bare, And _

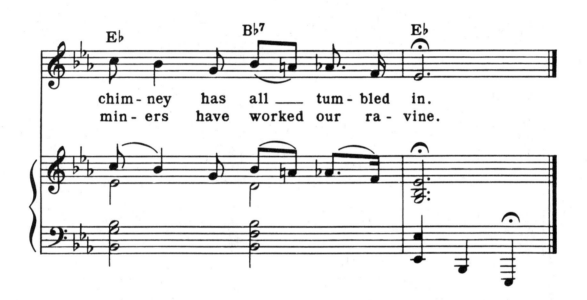

chim - ney   has   all ___ tum - bled in.
min - ers   have   worked our ra - vine.

3. Oh, don't you remember the mountains of snow,
   In sight from the camp all the year,
   And the valleys so green, where the wild flowers grow,
   And where we went hunting the deer?
   The cool little brook where we used to drink,
   Will always be running the same
   As when we were talking of home on the brink,
   Or cursing the day that we came.

4. Oh, don't you remember the well-beaten trail
   That led from the camp to the spring,
   And the potpies we made of the squirrel and quail,
   And the evenings when we used to sing?
   The trail and the spring we shall see them no more,
   Though never forget till we die;
   The shady old camp, with the ground for a floor,
   Forever, we bid thee good-by!

SHENANDOAH

Slow (free in delivery)

1. The old Miz-zoo, ___ she's a might-y riv-er. ___
2. The white man loved ___ an In-dian maid-en. ___

'Way ___ you roll-ing riv-er! ___ The
'Way ___ you roll-ing riv-er! ___ With

In-dians camp a-long her bor-der. ___ A-
no-tions his ca-noe was la-den. ___

way _____ we're bound, a - way, 'cross the wide _____ Mis - sou - ri. _____

3. Oh, Shenandoah, I love your daughter,
   'Way you rolling river,
   I'll take her 'cross your rolling water,
   Away, we're bound away, across the wide Missouri.

4. The Chief disdained the trader's dollars,
   'Way you rolling river,
   My daughter you shall never follow,
   Away, we're bound away, across the wide Missouri.

5. At last there came a Yankee skipper,
   'Way you rolling river,
   He winked his eye and he tipped his flipper,
   Away, we're bound away, across the wide Missouri.

6. He sold the chief that firewater,
   'Way you rolling river,
   And 'cross that river he stole his daughter,
   Away, we're bound away, across the wide Missouri.

7. Fare you well, I'm bound to leave you,
   'Way you rolling river,
   Oh Shenandoah I'll not deceive you,
   Away, we're bound away, across the wide Missouri.

SANTY ANNA

Slow and melancholy

1. O have you heard the lat - est _
2. O San - ty An - na fought for _

news? Heave a - way, San - ty An - na! ___ The
fame, Heave a - way, San - ty An - na! ___ He

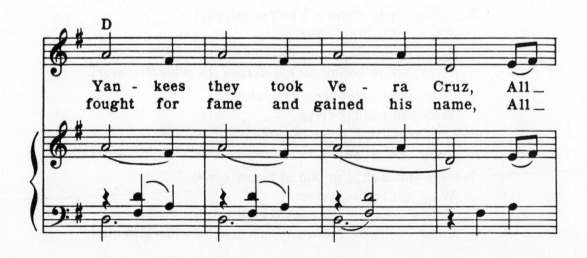

Yan - kees they took Ve - ra Cruz, All _
fought for fame and gained his name, All _

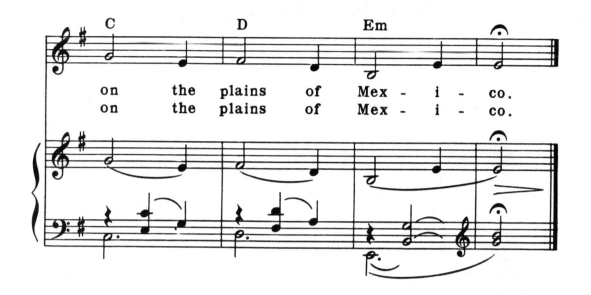

on   the   plains   of   Mex - i - co.
on   the   plains   of   Mex - i - co.

3. Old Santy Anna had a wooden leg,
   Heave away, Santy Anna!
   He used it for a wooden peg,
   All on the plains of Mexico!

4. Brave General Taylor gained the day,
   Heave away, Santy Anna!
   And Santy Anna run away,
   All on the plains of Mexico!

5. Ah, then we smashed them up and down;
   Heave away, Santy Anna!
   We captured all of that Mexican ground,
   All on the plains of Mexico!

6. The ladies there I do adore,
   Heave away, Santy Anna!
   I always want to be ashore,
   All on the plains of Mexico!

7. You've loved me dear and you've taught me well,
   Heave away, Santy Anna!
   I'd rather be here than frying in Hell,
   All on the plains of Mexico!

JESSE JAMES

Fast and with an exciting beat

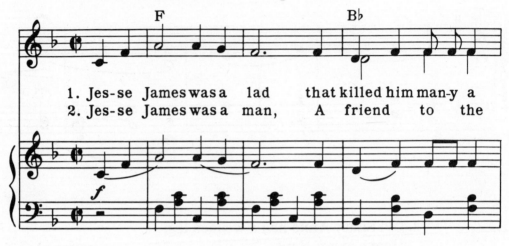

1. Jes-se James was a lad that killed him man-y a
2. Jes-se James was a man, A friend to the

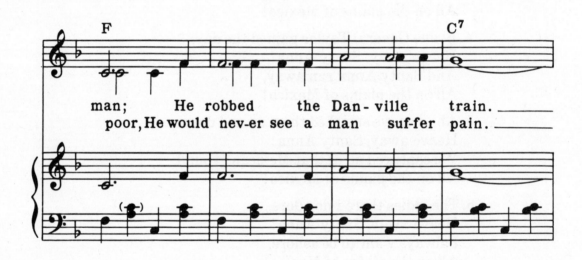

man; He robbed the Dan - ville train. _____
poor, He would nev-er see a man suf-fer pain. _____

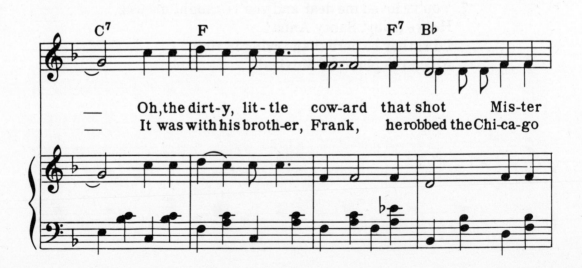

Oh, the dirt-y, lit-tle cow-ard that shot Mis-ter
It was with his broth-er, Frank, he robbed the Chi-ca-go

How-ard, Has laid poor Jes-se in his grave._____
bank,And he stopped the Glen - dale_ bank._____

CHORUS:

Poor Jes - se had a wife to mourn for his

life, The chil - dren they were brave._____

_____ But that dirt-y, lit-tle cow-ard that shot at Mis-ter

199

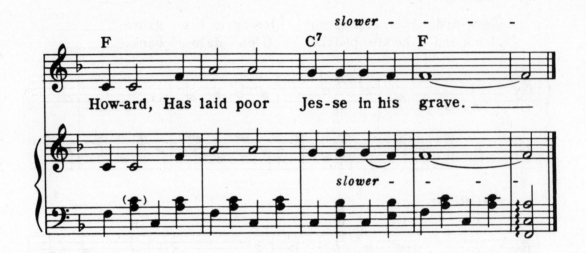

Howard, Has laid poor Jesse in his grave.

3. Oh, the people held their breath
   When they heard of Jesse's death
   And wondered how he came to die.
   It was one of the gang,
   Called little Robert Ford,
   He shot poor Jesse on the sly.
   Chorus

TOM DOOLEY

Slow

Hang down your head, Tom Doo - ley,

Hang down your head and cry, Hang down your head, Tom

Doo - ley, poor boy, you're go - ing to die.

2. I met her on the mountain,
  And there I took her life;
  I met her on the mountain
  And stabbed her with my knife.

3. This time tomorrow
  Know just where I'll be?
  In some lonesome valley,
  Hanging from a white oak tree.

4. Hang down your head, Tom Dooley,
  Hang down your head and cry,
  Hang down your head, Tom Dooley,
  Poor boy, you're going to die.

BILLY THE KID

Not too slow

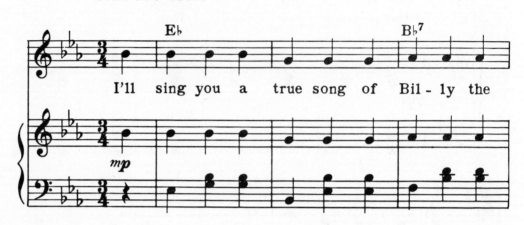

I'll sing you a true song of Bil - ly the

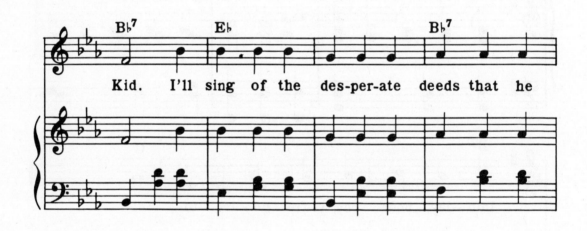

Kid. I'll sing of the des-per-ate deeds that he

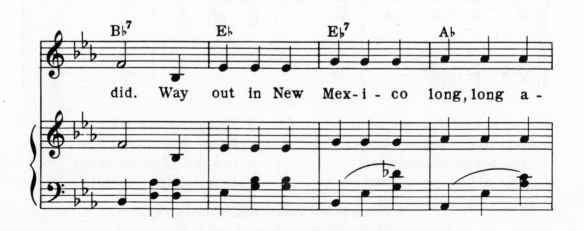

did. Way out in New Mex-i-co long, long a-

go, When a man's on-ly help was his own for-ty four.

2. When Billy the Kid was a very young lad,
   In old Silver City he went to the bad.
   Way out in the West with a gun in his hand,
   At the age of twelve years he killed his first man.

3. Fair Mexican maidens play guitars and sing
   A song about Billy, their boy bandit king,
   Who ere his young manhood had reached his sad end;
   He'd a notch on his pistol for twenty-one men.

4. 'Twas on the same night when poor Billy died,
   He said to his friends, "I'm not satisfied.
   There is twenty-one men I have put bullets through,
   And Sheriff Pat Garrett must make twenty-two."

5. Now this is how Billy the Kid met his fate:
   The bright moon was shinin', the hour was late,
   Shot down by Pat Garrett who once was his friend,
   The young outlaw's life had come to an end.

6. There's many a man with a face fine and fair
   Who starts out in life with a chance to be square,
   But just like poor Billy he wanders astray
   And loses his life in the very same way.

GIT ALONG, LITTLE DOGIES

Easy-going waltz

As I was a-walk-ing one morn - ing for

pleas-ure, ____ Spied a cow-punch-er a - rid-ing a -

long. _____ His hat was throwed

back and his spurs ___ was a- jin - glin'; ___

As he ap-proached he was a-sing-in' this song. ___ "Whoopee

CHORUS:

ti - yi - yay, _____ Git a - long ___

___ lit-tle do-gies, ___ It's your mis - for-tune and

COWBOY'S DREAM

In a waltz rhythm

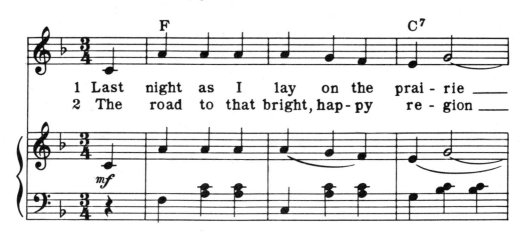

1 Last night as I lay on the prai - rie ____
2 The road to that bright, hap - py re - gion ____

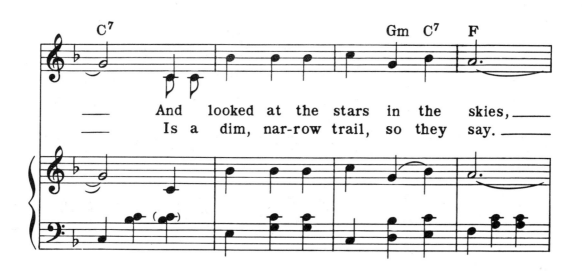

____ And looked at the stars in the skies, ____
____ Is a dim, nar-row trail, so they say. ____

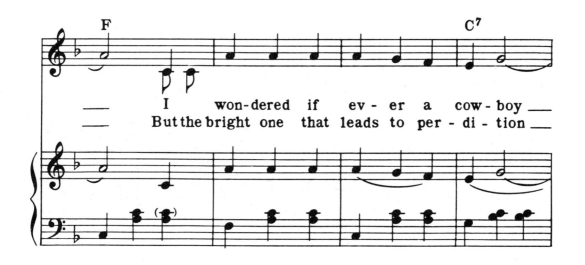

____ I won-dered if ev - er a cow - boy ____
____ But the bright one that leads to per - di - tion ____

COWBOY'S DREAM

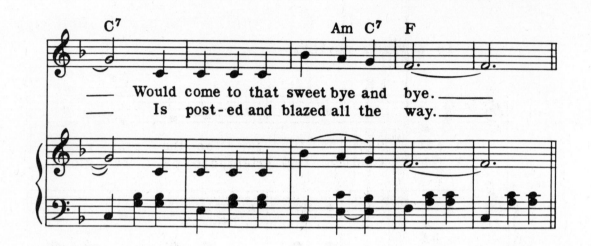

Would come to that sweet bye and bye._____
Is post-ed and blazed all the way._____

CHORUS:

Roll on, roll on, ___ Roll

on lit-tle do-gie, roll on, roll on.

Roll on, roll on,___ Roll

on lit-tle do-gie, roll on.___

3. I wonder if ever a cowboy
   Stood ready for that great judgment day
   And could say to the boss of the riders:
   "I'm ready, come drive me away."
   Chorus

4. But they tell of another big owner
   Who's ne'er o'er-stocked, so they say,
   But who always makes room for the sinners
   Who drift from the straight narrow way.
   Chorus

5. But to be shipped to that bright, mystic region,
   Over there in green pastures to lie,
   And be led by the crystal, still waters
   To that home in the sweet Bye-and-Bye.
   Chorus

OLD PAINT

A slow waltz

I ride an old paint, I lead old Dan, I'm a-
go - ing to Mon-tan' for to throw the hool-i- han. They
feed in the cou-lee, they wa - ter in the draw, Their
tails are all mat-ted, their backs are all raw. Ride a-

round, lit-tle do-gie, Ride a - round 'em slow;— The fier - y and the snuf-fy are a - rar-in' to go.

2. Old Bill Jones had two daughters and a song;
One went to Denver, the other went wrong;
His wife, she died in a poolroom fight,
But still he keeps on singin' from morning to night.
Chorus

3. When I die, take my saddle from the wall;
Lead out my pony, lead him out of his stall;
Tie my bones to the saddle, turn his face toward the West,
And we'll ride the prairie that we love the best.
Chorus

LAVENDER COWBOY

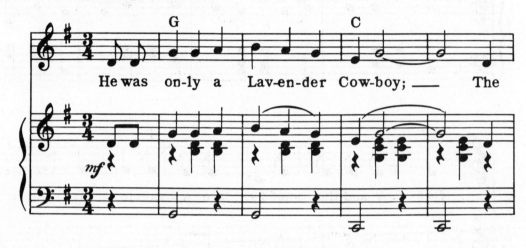

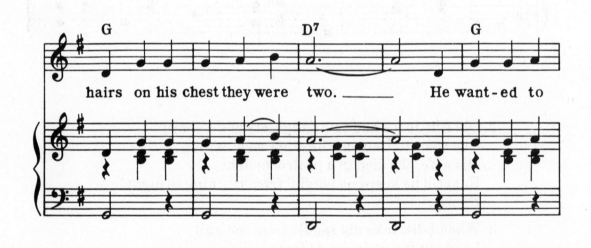

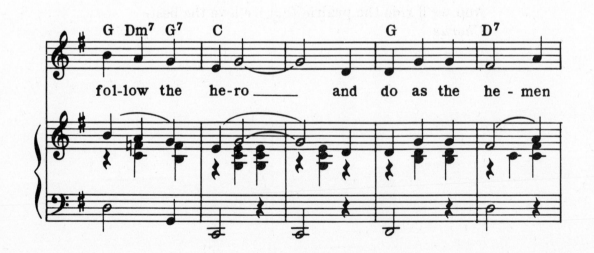

2. Red, green, and many-colored hair tonics,
   He rubbed on his chest day and night;
   When he looked in the mirror next morning,
   No new hairs grew in sight.

3. He battled for Red Nellie's honor,
   He cleaned up a hold-up nest;
   He died with two six-guns a-smokin',
   But only two hairs on his chest.

THE COWBOY'S LAMENT

Waltz, rather slow

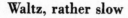

1. As I___ walked out in the streets of La-
2. "I see by your out-fit that you are a

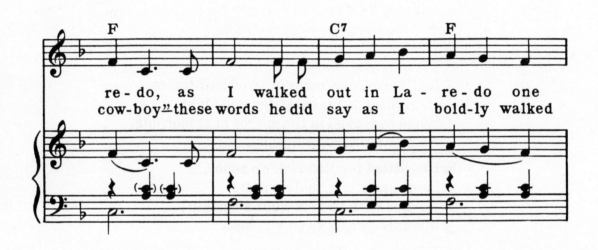

re-do, as I walked out in La-re-do one
cow-boy," these words he did say as I bold-ly walked

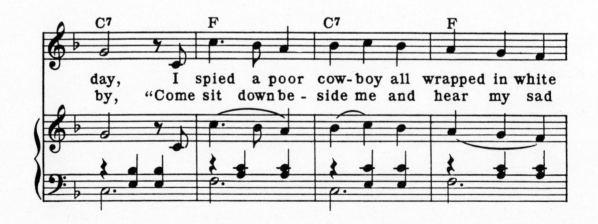

day, I spied a poor cow-boy all wrapped in white
by, "Come sit down be-side me and hear my sad

214

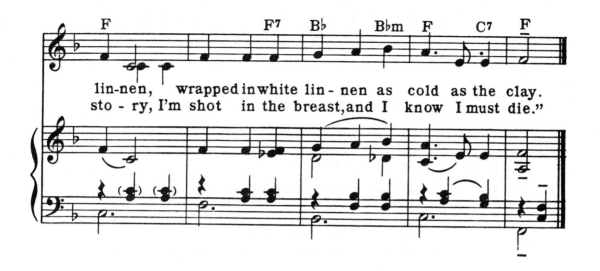

lin-nen, wrapped in white lin-nen as cold as the clay.
sto-ry, I'm shot in the breast, and I know I must die."

3. "It was once in the saddle I used to go dashing,
   Once in the saddle I used to go gay,
   First down to Rosie's and then to the card house,
   Shot in the breast and I'm dying today.

4. "Get sixteen gamblers to carry my coffin
   Six purty maidens to sing me a song;
   Take me to the valley and lay the sod o'er me,
   For I'm a young cowboy an' know I done wrong.

5. "O, beat the drum slowly and play the fife lowly,
   Play the dead march as they carry me along,
   Put bunches of roses all over my coffin,
   Roses to deaden the clods as they fall."

6. As I walked out in the streets of Laredo,
   As I walked out in Laredo one day,
   I spied a young cowboy all wrapped in white linen,
   Wrapped in white linen, as cold as the clay.

THE OLD CHISHOLM TRAIL

With a happy beat - in 2

1. Come a-long boys and I'll tell you a tale,
start-ed up the trail, Oc - to-ber twen-ty-third,

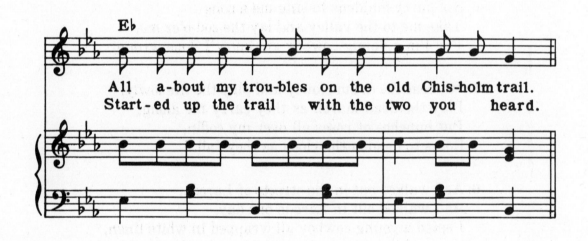

All a-bout my trou-bles on the old Chis-holm trail.
Start-ed up the trail with the two you heard.

CHORUS:

Come - a ti - yi - yip - pi, Come - a

ti-yi - yay,　　Ti - yi - yip-pi, yi - yay.　　2. I

3. On a ten-dollar hoss and a forty-dollar saddle,
   Gittin' tired of punchin' your dad-gum cattle.
   Chorus

4. Jumped in the saddle and I grabbed a-hold the horn,
   The best darn' cowboy that ever was born.
   Chorus

5. It's cloudy in the West and it looks like rain,
   The darn'd old slicker's in the wagon again.
   Chorus

6. It begin to storm and the rain begin to fall,
   And we thought, by grab, we're a-goin' to lose 'em all.
   Chorus

7. We hit the Caldwell, we hit her on the fly,
   And we bedded down the cattle on the hills close by.
   Chorus

RED RIVER VALLEY

With a cowboy rhythm—in 4

1. From this val-ley they say you are go-ing,___ We will
2. Won't you think of the val-ley you're leav-ing?___ Oh, how

mp

miss your bright eyes and sweet smile, For they
lone - ly, how sad it will be. Oh,___

say you are tak - ing the sun-shine___ That
think of the fond heart you're break-ing,___ And the

bright - ens our path - way a while.
grief you are caus - ing me to see.

CHORUS:

Come and sit by my side if you love me.___ Do not

has - ten to bid me a - dieu, But re -

mem - ber the Red Riv - er Val - ley_____ And the

girl who has loved you so true.

3. From this valley they say you are going;
   When you go, may your darling go too?
   Would you leave her behind unprotected
   When she loves no other but you?
   Chorus

4. As you go to your home by the ocean,
   May you never forget those sweet hours
   That we spent in the Red River Valley
   And the love we exchanged 'mid the flowers.
   Chorus

MIDNIGHT SPECIAL

1. Yon-der comes Miss Ro-sie, _____ How'n the world do you
2. Lord, Thel-ma says she loves me, _____ But I b'lieve she told a

know? _____ I can tell her by her a - pron _____
lie, _____ 'Cause she has-n't been to see me _____

_____ and the dress she wore. _____ Um-brel-la on her
_____ since last Ju - ly. _____ She brought me a lit-tle

221

shoul-der,_____ Piece of pa-per in her hand,_____
cof-fee,_____ She brought me a lit-tle tea._____

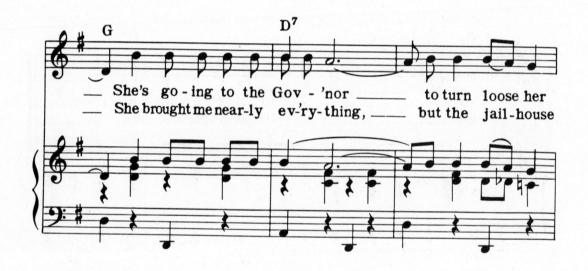

___ She's go-ing to the Gov - 'nor _____ to turn loose her
She brought me near-ly ev-'ry-thing, ___ but the jail-house

CHORUS:

man._____
key._____ Let the mid-night spe-cial _____

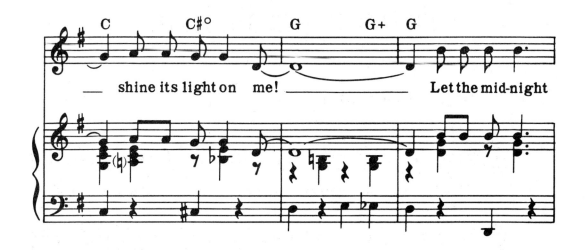

shine its light on me! _____ Let the mid-night

spe-cial _____ shine its ev-er-lov-in' light on me. _____

3. When you wake up in the morning, boy,
   You hear the ding-dong ring.
   When you go to the table,
   You'll find the same durn thing.

4. Knife and fork on the table,
   Nothing in your pan;
   If you say anything about it,
   You'll have trouble with that man.
   Chorus

5. If you ever go to Houston, boy,
   Hey, you'd better act right;
   You'd better not gamble,
   And you'd better not fight.

6. For the sheriff will arrest you,
   And the boys will take you down,
   And the next thing you know,
   You're prison bound.
   Chorus

FRANKIE AND JOHNNIE

With a fast beat -in 2

Frank-ie and John-nie were lov-ers,   Oh, how they did

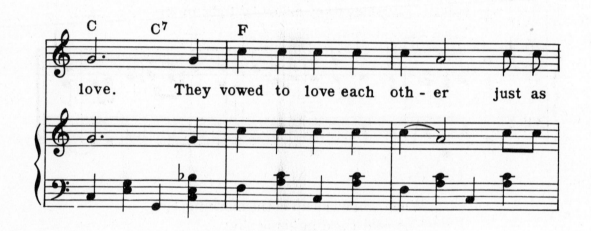

love.   They vowed to love each oth - er   just as

long as there were stars a - bove. _ He was her man; _

Would-n't do her wrong. _____

2. Frankie went down to the corner,
   To get a bucket of beer.
   She said, "Oh, Mr. Bartender,
   Has my loving Johnnie been here?
   He's my man; wouldn't do me wrong."

3. "Don't want to cause you no trouble,
   Don't want to tell you no lies;
   Saw your man half an hour ago
   Making love to Nellye Blye;
   He's your man all right, but he's doing you wrong."

4. Frankie went down to the drugstore;
   She went to buy a gun.
   She said, "Oh, Mr. Drug Store Man,
   I want that big and shiny one,
   He's my man and he's doing me wrong."

5. Frankie pulled back her kimono,
   Pulled out her little forty-four,
   Roo-ta-ti-toot, three times she shot
   Right through that hard wood door.
   She shot her man 'cause he was doing her wrong.

6. "Roll me over on the left side,
   Roll me over slow.
   Roll me over on the left side
   'Cause them bullets hurt me so.
   I was your man but I was doing you wrong."

7. It wasn't murder in the second degree,
   It wasn't murder in the third.
   Frankie just went and dropped her man,
   Like a hunter drops a bird.
   He was her man but he was doing her wrong.

8. Frankie went walking down Broadway
   The last day that she would be free.
   All she could hear was a three-string bow
   Playing "Nearer My God to Thee."
   He was her man but he was doing her wrong.

FARE THEE WELL, O HONEY (SAD MAN'S SONG)

Very free in delivery-slow

1. If I had wings, ___ like No-ah's dove, I'd fly up the riv-er to the girl I love.
2. I've got a girl and she's straight and tall, She moves her bod-y like a can-non ball.

Fare thee well, O Hon-ey, Fare thee well. ___

L.H. over

3. One of these nights,
   And it won't be long,
   I'll call her name
   And she'll be gone.
   Fare thee well, O Honey, fare thee well.

4. I remember one night
   In a drizzlin' rain,
   All around my heart
   I felt an achin' pain.
   Fare thee well, O Honey, fare thee well.

5. If I had wings,
   Like Noah's dove,
   I'd fly up the river
   To the girl I love.
   Fare thee well, O Honey, fare thee well.

BALLAD OF JOHN HENRY

With a driving rhythm

1. When John Hen-ry was a lit-tle ba-by, ___ A-
2. John Hen-ry had a lit-tle wom-an, ___ Her

set-tin' on his pap-py's knee, He
name was Mar - y Anne. When John

gave one, long___ and lone-some cry;___ Said:"This
Hen-ry was sick___ and a-lay-in' in bed,___ Mar - y

3. The captain said to John Henry:
"Gonna bring me a steam drill 'round!
Gonna take that steam drill out on the job;
I'm gonna whup that steel on down,
I'm gonna whup that steel on down."

4. The man that invented the steam drill,
He thought he was mighty fine.
John Henry drove a hundred and fifty feet;
The steam drill a hundred and nine!
The steam drill a hundred and nine.

5. The captain said to John Henry:
"I believe this mountain's cavin' in."
John Henry gave one long and lonesome cry,
"Why, it's only my hammer suckin' wind,
It's only my hammer suckin' wind."

6. Then the captain said to John Henry:
"John Henry, why don't you sing?"
"I'm a-throwin' twelve pounds from my hips on down;
Listen to the cold steel ring,
Listen to the cold steel ring."

7. John Henry was a-hammerin' on the mountain
And his hammer was a-strikin' fire,
He drove so hard that he broke his poor heart;
He laid down his hammer and he died,
He laid down his hammer and he died.

8. John Henry had another little woman,
And the dress she wore was blue.
The very last words she said to him was,
"Honey, I've been true to you,
Honey, I've been true to you."

9. "Then where did you get that dress, gal?
Where did you get those shoes so fine?"
"I got the dress from off a railroad man,
And the shoes from a driver in the mine,
The shoes from a driver in the mine."

10. They took John Henry to the White House,
And they buried him 'neath the sand;
And every locomotive comes a-rollin' by
Says: "There lies a steel drivin' man,
There lies a steel drivin' man."

BIG ROCK CANDY MOUNTAIN

In a gay rhythm

Oh, the buz-zin' of the bees, and the cig-a-rette trees, The so-da wa - ter foun-tain, Where the lem-on-ade springs and the blue-bird sings In that Big Rock Can-dy Moun-tain.

The end

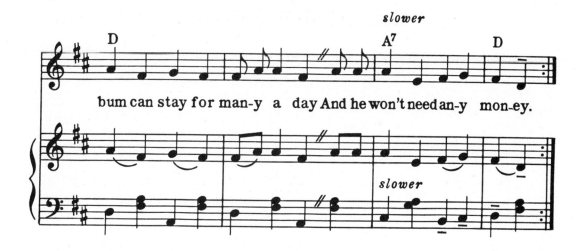

bum can stay for man-y a day And he won't need an-y mon-ey.

2. In the Big Rock Candy Mountain, the cops have wooden legs,
   The bulldogs all have rubber teeth and the hens lay soft-boiled eggs.
   The farmer's trees are full of fruit, the barns are full of hay,

   *I wanna go where their ain't no snow, where the sleet don't fall
   and the wind don't blow**
   In that Big Rock Candy Mountain.
   Chorus

   ——————
   *Free interpolation.

ST. JOHN'S RIVER

Free in delivery

*Left hand continues in a soft rhythm. Melody floats on top like a chant.

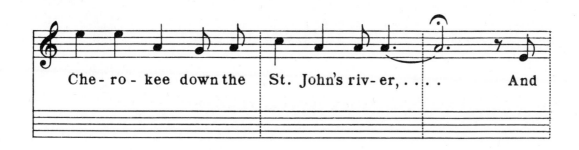

Che - ro - kee down the St. John's riv - er, ... And

na - ry a cent will I be the giv - er. ....

CRAWDAD SONG

Fast and with a driving rhythm

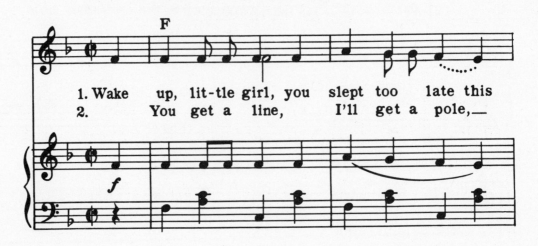

1. Wake up, lit-tle girl, you slept too late this
2. You get a line, I'll get a pole,—

morn-ing; ——— Wake up, lit-tle girl, you slept too late, babe.
hon-ey, ——— You get a line, I'll get a pole, babe.

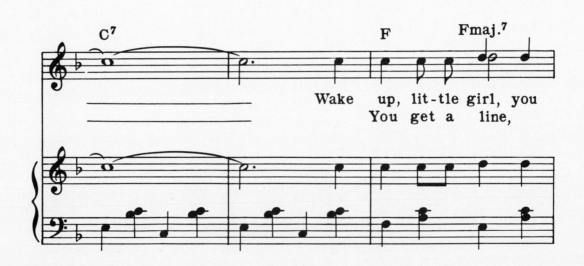

Wake up, lit-tle girl, you
You get a line,

slept too late. The craw-dad man just passed your gate this
I'll get a pole, I'll meet you down by the craw-dad hole;

morn-ing, this eve-ning, so soon.
hon-ey, babe of mine.

3. Put your hand on your hip, let your mind roll by, honey,
   Put your hand on your hip, let your mind roll by, babe,
   Put your hand on your hip, let your mind roll by,
   'Cause your body gotta swivel when you come to die;
   Honey, babe of mine.

4. Settin' on the ice, feet got cold, honey,
   Settin' on the ice, feet got cold, babe,
   Settin' on the ice, feet got cold,
   Watchin' that crawdad dig his hole;
   Honey, babe of mine.

5. Settin' on the bank, feet got hot, honey,
   Settin' on the bank, feet got hot, babe,
   Settin' on the bank, feet got hot,
   Watchin' that crawdad rack and trot;
   Honey, babe of mine.

6. Old crawdad, you better dig deep, honey,
   Old crawdad, you better dig deep, babe,
   Old crawdad, you better dig deep,
   'Cause I'm gonna ramble in my sleep;
   Honey, babe of mine.

WANDERIN'

Free in delivery-slow

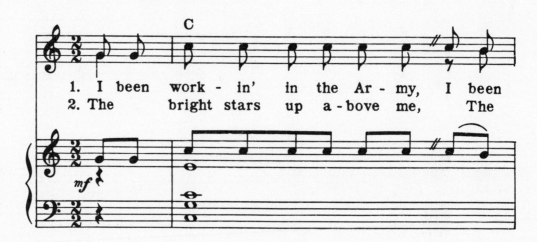

1. I been work - in' in the Ar - my, I been
2. The bright stars up a - bove me, The

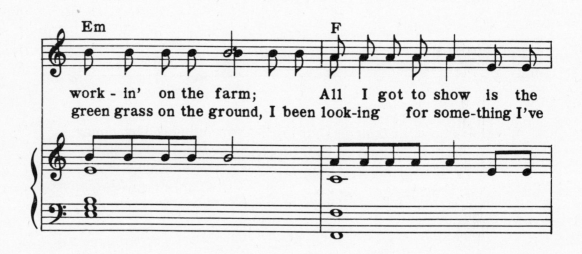

work - in' on the farm; All I got to show is the
green grass on the ground, I been look-ing for some-thing I've

mus - cles in my arm. And it looks like I'm
nev - er ___ found, And it looks like I'm

nev - er gon - na cease my wan - der - in'. ___

3. I been travelin' early.
   I been travelin' late,
   From New York City to the Golden Gate;
   And it looks like I'm never gonna cease my wanderin'.

I'M GOING DOWN THE ROAD

Fast and with a driving rhythm

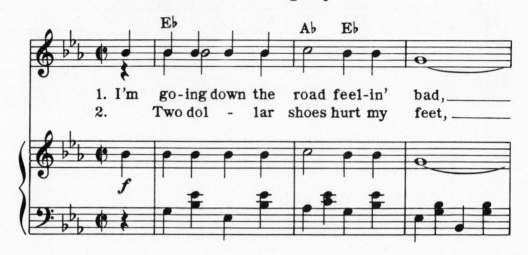

1. I'm go-ing down the road feel-in' bad,_____
2. Two dol - lar shoes hurt my feet,_____

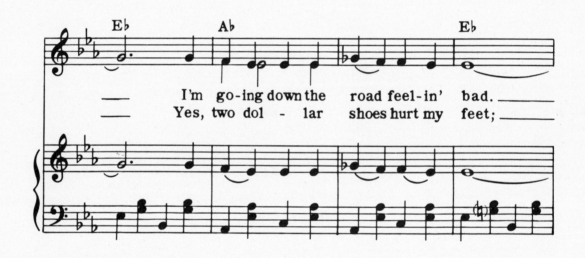

—— I'm go-ing down the road feel-in' bad.——
—— Yes, two dol - lar shoes hurt my feet;——

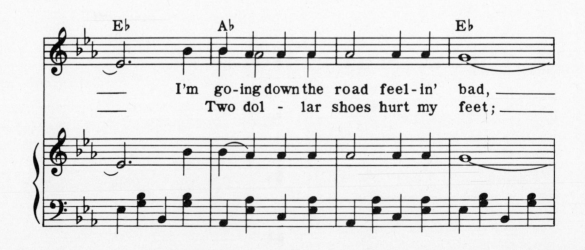

—— I'm go-ing down the road feel-in' bad,_____
—— Two dol - lar shoes hurt my feet;_____

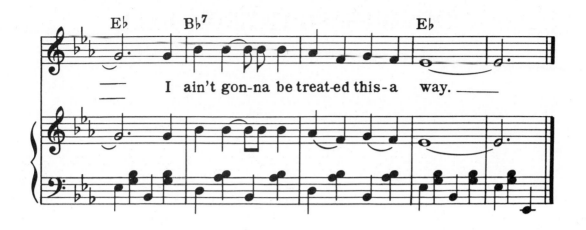

I ain't gon-na be treat-ed this-a way. ———

3. Takes a ten-dollar shoe to fit my feet,
   Takes a ten-dollar shoe to fit my feet,
   Ten-dollar shoe to fit my feet;
   I ain't gonna be treated this-a way.

4. I'm going where the water tastes like wine,
   Going where the water tastes like wine,
   Kansas water tastes like turpentine;
   I ain't gonna be treated this-a way.

5. I'm going where the climate suits my clothes,
   I'm going where the climate suits my clothes,
   Going where the climate suits my clothes;
   I ain't gonna be treated this-away.

THE WABASH CANNON BALL

(THE CANNON BALL TO HEAVEN)

With a swinging beat - in 2

From the waves of the At - lan - tic to the wild Pa - cif - ic shore. From the coast of Cal - i - for - nia to ice-bound Lab-ra - dor. There's a train, a su - per

fli - er, O, hear her thrill - ing call, "All a-
board, ye tired ho-boes, It's the Wa-bash Can-non Ball."

2. O, listen to the rumble, O, listen to the roar,
   As she echoes down the valley and tears along the shore.
   Hear the engine thunder, hear her mighty whistle call;
   There's mulligan in the club car of the Wabash Cannon Ball.

3. All the greatest cities, we'll pass through on our way:
   Chicago, Minneapolis, Des Moines, Santa Fe,
   Springfield and Decatur, Saint Louis, Montreal;
   Through Mobile and Chattanooga on the Wabash Cannon Ball.

4. A fond farewell to Memphis, Atlanta, Mexico,
   Dallas and El Paso, boys, we won't be goin' slow,
   The mighty Rocky Mountains, where rushing waters fall;
   There'll be no bulls or brakemen on the Wabash Cannon Ball.

5. There are other places, partner; we will give a final look
   To Terre Haute and Dayton, Kansas City, Keokuk.
   Like a flash we'll travel upward, out of sight the earth will fall,
   As we travel straight to glory on the Wabash Cannon Ball.

6. On arrival at the station, this train will not be late
   To attend Saint Pete's reception just beside the pearly gate;
   "Well done, my faithful servants," we'll hear the Master call,
   "Welcome to all passengers of the Wabash Cannon Ball."

7. O, listen to the rumble, O, listen to the roar,
   As she echoes down the valley and tears along the shore.
   Hear the engine thunder, hear her mighty whistle call;
   There'll be rejoicing in the club car of the Wabash Cannon Ball.

NEWS STORIES IN SONG

There was a time when a hit song was not news, but news became a hit song. Battle reports would appear in verse form on the editorial pages of local newspapers (to be reprinted in the newspapers of one colonial town after another until known the length and breadth of the land) or on separate song sheets known as "broadsides."

A story in verse and music fulfilled the function of today's newspaper, radio, or television screen, giving information with dramatic interest and entertainment.

History and social events come alive when documented with examples that reach down to the level of individual experience. What one immediately recognizes in a folk song is the basic immediacy which gives the song its strength. These songs relate as a personal experience what on a larger scale can be regarded as a major historical trend or event. One would not want to reproduce or sing all of the songs created and sung during those years, but a chronological arrangement of the best of these presents a bird's-eye view of American history, as well as some interesting songs for today.

Songs were used as a means of bringing recruits to the Revolutionary cause and of keeping morale high. Barlow, the Hartford poet, entering the Revolutionary Army as Chaplain, wrote: "I do not know whether I shall do more for the cause in the capacity of Chaplain, than I would in that of Poet; I have great faith in the influence of songs; and I shall continue, while fulfilling the duties of my appointment, to write one now and then, and to encourage the taste for them which I find in the camp."

The poet, the satirist, and the writer of songs employed his wit in writing patriotic songs for the Revolutionary War and the War of 1812. These songs meant something in our country's development and mean something today. They are important not only for content, but for the spirit that caused them to be written.

After the War of 1812, the expansion of our country involved fighting with the Indians and with the Mexicans. When General Jackson defeated the Creeks in Alabama or a battle was fought with the Sioux in Oregon, reports in song were popular with soldiers and civilians. After these battles, the same songs became fixtures with settlers and cowboys.

The Civil War produced more songs than any war in our country's history, except perhaps World War I. There were marching songs, sentimental songs, songs for recruiting, humorous songs, and the many songs, by writers both known and anonymous, that expressed the feelings and revealed the life of the people of our disunited country.

After the Civil War, we find that songs were, for the most part, no longer of the same quality. Songs of the Spanish-American War and World Wars I and II are of a different quality and have less of a "folk" utility, as we have herein defined folk.

Our historical songs are a moving and meaningful part of our musical heritage. They are good singing and they express something of the thinking and vitality that makes America strong.

1759-1812
HOW HAPPY THE SOLDIER
(WHY SOLDIER WHY)

*This favorite of the British soldiers during the Rev-
olutionary War was picked up by the Americans.
It was sung by both sides during the War of 1812.*

1. How hap-py the sol-dier who lives on his pay,   and
2. He cares not a Mar-ne-dy how the world goes; his

spends half a crown__ on six-pence a day;   he
King finds his quar-ters, and mon-ey and clothes;   he

fears nei-ther jus-tic-es,   war-rants, nor bums, but
laughs at all sor-row when-ev-er it comes, and

pays all his debts with a roll of his drums, with a
ratt-les a-way with the roll of his drums, with a

row de dow, row de dow, row de dow, dow, and he

pays all his debts with a roll of his drums.

3. The drum is his glory, his joy, and delight,
   It leads him to pleasure as well as to fight;
   No girl, when she hears it, though ever so glum,
   But packs up her tatters, and follows the drum.
   With row de dow, row de dow, row de dow, dow;
   And he pays all his debts with the roll of his drums.

THE LIBERTY SONG

In 1768, John Dickinson of Delaware, later a member of the first Congress, wrote this song to the English tune "Heart of Oak." It became widely known, reprinted as a broadside and in newspapers, and sung in the taverns.

1. Come, join hand in hand, brave A- mer - i-cans all, And
2. Our wor-thy fore-fa- thers, let's give them a cheer, To

rouse your bold hearts at fair Lib - er- ty's call; No __
cli- mates un- known did cou - ra- geous-ly steer: Through

tyr - an-nous act shall sup-press your just claim, Or
o - ceans, to des - erts, for free- dom they came, And

stain with dis - hon - or   A - mer - i - ca's name;
dy - ing, be-queath'd us their free - dom and fame. In

CHORUS:

free - dom we're born and in free - dom we'll live; Our

purs - es are read - y,   Stead - y, friends, stead - y, Not as

THE LIBERTY SONG

slaves but as free men our mon-ey we'll give.

3. The tree their own hands had to liberty rear'd
   They lived to behold growing strong and rever'd;
   With transport they cry'd, "Now our witness we gain,
   For our children shall gather the fruits of our pain."
   Chorus

4. All ages shall speak with amaze and applause
   Of the courage we'll show in support of our laws;
   To die we can bear, but serve we disdain,
   For shame is to freedom more dreadful than pain.
   Chorus

THE BATTLE SONG OF SARATOGA

General Burgoyne and his German mercenaries (Hessians) surrendered at Saratoga, New York, October 1777. The account in this song is set to the familiar Irish melody, "Brennan on the Moor."

Steady, in 2

1. Come un - to me, ye he-roes, and I the truth will tell __ con-
2. Be - fore the Ti-con-der-o - ga, full well both night and day __ their

cern-ing man-y a sol - dier who for his coun-try fell. __ Bur-
mo-tions we ob - served __ be-fore the blood-y fray; __ Bur-

goyne, the King's com-mand - er and curs-èd To - ry crew, __ with
goyne sent Baum to Benn-ing-ton, with Hes-sians there he went, __ to

THE BATTLE SONG OF SARATOGA

3. But little did they know then
      with whom they had to deal.
   It was not quite so easy
      our stores and stocks to steal.
   Stark would give them only
      a portion of his lead,
   With half his crew ere sunset,
      Baum lay among the dead.

4. The 19th of September,
      the morning cool and clear,
   Gates addressed the army
      each soldier's heart to cheer.
   "Burgoyne," he cried, "advances,
      but we will never fly,
   But rather than surrender,
      we'll fight him till we die!"

5. The Seventh of October,
      they did capitulate,
   Burgoyne and his proud army
      we did our prisoners make.
   And vain was their endeavor
      our men to terrify,
   Though death was all around us,
      not one of us would fly!

6. Now here's a health to Herkimer
      and our commander Gates!
   To Freedom and to Washington
      whom every Tory hates.
   Likewise unto our Congress—
      God grant it long to reign—
   Our country, rights and justice
      forever to maintain!

BALLAD OF THE TEA PARTY

This ballad commemorates an historical event every American knows well. The melody, first heard in 1730, is from the old English sea song, "Come and Listen to My Ditty," or "The Sailor's Complaint."

Steady, in 2

1. Tea-ships near to Bos-ton ly - ing, on the wharf a num-er-ous crew. Sons of free-dom, nev - er dy - ing, then ap - peared in view! With a rink-tum, dink-tum,

2. Armed with ham-mers, ax - es, chi-sels, wea-pons new for war - like deed, toward the tax - èd, freight-ed ves - sels on they came with speed. With a rink-tum, dink-tum,

fa la link-tum, then ap-peared in view, With a
fa la link-tum, on they came with speed, With a

rink-tum,dink-tum,fa la link-tum,then ap-peared in view!
rink-tum,dink-tum,fa la link-tum, on they came with speed.

3. Overboard she goes, my boys,
　　heave—
Ho where darling waters roar:
We love our cup of tea full well but
Love our freedom more.

Chorus: With a rinktum, dinktum,
　　　　　fa la linktum,
　　　　　Love our freedom more.

4. Deep, into the sea descended
Curséd weed of China's coast;
Thus at once our fears were ended,
Rights shall ne'er be lost!

Chorus: With a rinktum, dinktum,
　　　　　fa la linktum,
　　　　　Rights shall ne'er be lost!

THE BOSTON TEA TAX

The tea-dumping affair in Boston Harbor has always tickled the imagination of Americans. Here's another song on the subject that began as a comedy number on the variety stage, proved to have staying power, and became a folk song.

Steady, in 2

1. I snum I am a Yan-kee lad, and I guess I'll sing a dit-ty;___ and_ if you do not rel-ish it, the more 'twill be the pit-y;_____ that

2. And t'oth-er day the Yan-kee folks were _ mad a-bout the tax-es,___ and_ so we went like In-juns dress'd to split tea chests with ax-es.___ It

3. And then a-board the ships we went our___ ven-geance to ad-min-is-ter, we _ did-n't care one tar-nal bit for an-y king or min-is-ter. We

is, I think I should have been a plague-y sight more
was the year of sev'n-ty-three and we felt real-ly
made a plague-y mess of tea in one of the big-gest

slower

fin-ished man. If __ I'd been born in Bos-ton town, but I
grit-ty. __ The May-or would have led the gang, but __
dish-es; __ I __ mean we steeped it in the sea and __

a tempo

warn't 'cause I'm a coun-try man.
Bos - ton warn't a ci - ty! Fol-de - rol - de-ray, Fol-de-
treat-ed all the fish - es.

but I warn't 'cause I'm a coun-try man.
rol - de -ray, but __ Bos - ton warn't a ci - ty!
and __ treat - ed all the fish - es.

FREE AMERICA

Americans embarked on the Revolutionary War in a militant optimistic spirit. The writer of this song, Dr. Joseph Warren of Boston, one of the original minutemen, was killed at Bunker Hill. He used the melody of a well-known English song, "The British Grenadier."

Martial (heavy accents on every beat)

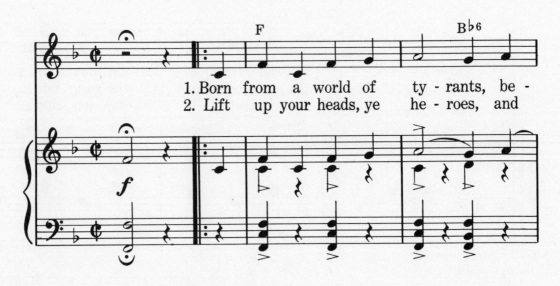

1. Born from a world of ty-rants, be-
2. Lift up your heads, ye he-roes, and

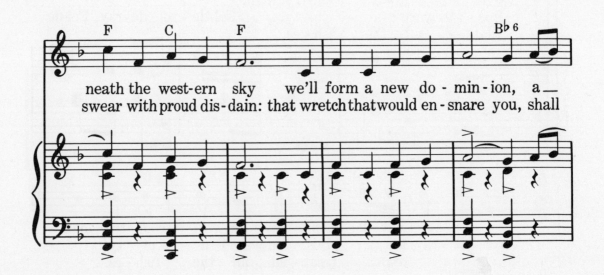

neath the west-ern sky we'll form a new do-min-ion, a —
swear with proud dis-dain: that wretch that would en-snare you, shall

land of lib - er - ty. The world shall own we're
lay his snares in vain. Should Eu - rope emp - ty

mas - ters here, then has - ten on the day:___ op -
all her force, we'll meet her in ar - ray,___ and

pose, op - pose, op - pose, op - pose, for North A - mer - i - cay.
fight and shout, and shout and fight for North A - mer - i - cay.

3. We led fair freedom hither,
   And lo, the desert smiled!
   A paradise of pleasure
   Was opened in the wild!
   Your harvest, bold Americans,
   No power shall snatch away!
   Huzza, huzza, huzza, huzza,
   For Free America.

CHESTER

New England congregations were social as well as religious centers. They sang secular hymns and, as tension grew with England, patriotic ones too. "Chester," written by William Billings, the early New England composer, became a marching song for the Revolutionary soldiers.

Like a march (not too slow)

1. Let ty-rants shake their i-ron___ rod,
2. Howe and Bur-goyne and Clin-ton,___ too,
3. When God in-spired us for__ the__ fight,

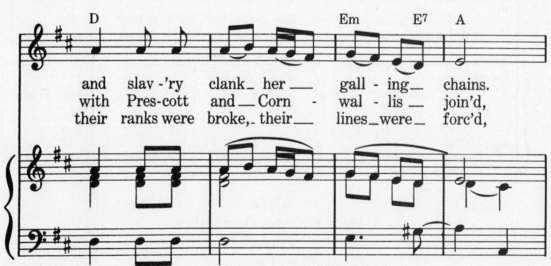

and slav-'ry clank__ her __ gall-ing__ chains.
with Pres-cott and__ Corn - wal-lis __ join'd,
their ranks were broke,_ their__ lines_were_ forc'd,

We'll fear them not; we trust in God:
to - geth - er plot our o - ver - throw,
their ships were shel - ter'd in our sight,

New England's God for - ev - er reigns.
in one in - fer - nal league com - bin'd.
or swift - ly driv - en from our coast.

4. The foe comes on with haughty stride,
   Our troops advance with martial noise,
   Their vet'rans flee before our youth,
   And generals yield to beardless boys.

5. What grateful offering shall we bring,
   What shall we render to the Lord?
   Loud hallelujahs let us sing,
   And praise His name on every chord.

THE RIFLEMEN'S SONG AT BENNINGTON

General Burgoyne's disasters, en route from Canada to Albany by way of Lake Champlain, were recorded in popular contemporary ballads. At Bennington one of his foraging detachments was surrounded. The disastrous outcome resulted in this mocking ballad.

Like a March

1. Why come ye hith-er, Red-coats, your mind what mad-ness fills? In our val-leys there is dan-ger, and there's dan-ger on our hills. Oh, hear ye not the

2. Ye ride a good-ly steed, ye may know an-oth-er mas-ter. Ye for-ward came with speed, but you'll learn to back much fas-ter. Then you'll meet our Moun-tain

3. Tell he who stays at home, or cross the brin-y wa-ters, that thith-er ye must come, like bul-locks to the slaugh-ter. If we the work must

sing - ing of the bu - gle wild and free? and
Boys and their lead - er, John - ny Stark, lads who
do, why, the soon - er 'tis be - gun, if

soon you'll know the ring - ing of the ri - fle from the tree.
make but lit - tle noise, but who al - ways hit the mark.
flint and trig - ger hold but true, the soon - er 'twill be done.

CHORUS

Oh, the ri - fle, _____ oh, the ri - fle _____ in our

hands will prove no tri - fle. _____

YANKEE MAN O' WAR

The most famous naval commander of the American Revolution was John Paul Jones. His raids inspired this ballad, glorifying his skill in outmaneuvering the enemy.

Like a march

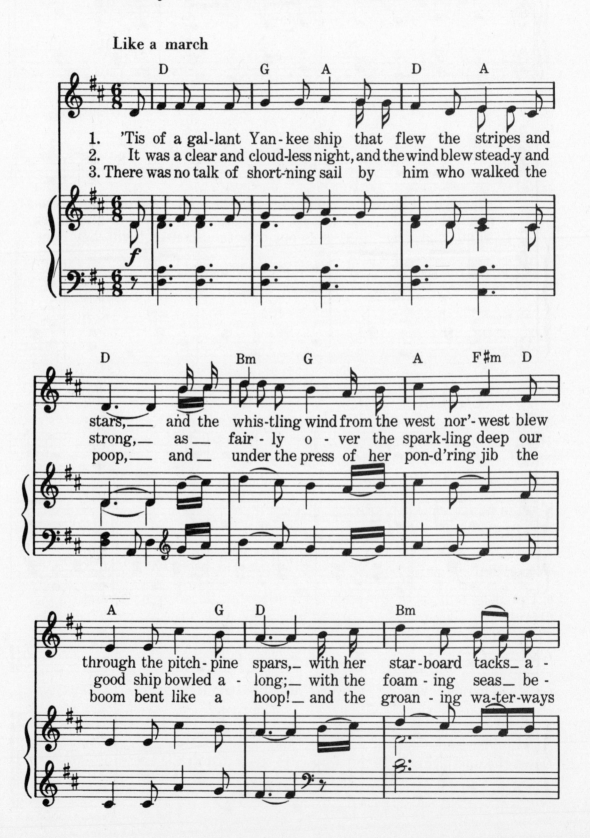

1. 'Tis of a gal-lant Yan-kee ship that flew the stripes and
2. It was a clear and cloud-less night, and the wind blew stead-y and
3. There was no talk of short-ning sail by him who walked the

stars,___ and the whis-tling wind from the west nor'-west blew
strong,___ as___ fair - ly o - ver the spark-ling deep our
poop,___ and___ under the press of her pon-d'ring jib the

through the pitch-pine spars,_ with her star-board tacks_ a -
good ship bowled a - long;_ with the foam - ing seas_ be -
boom bent like a hoop!_ and the groan - ing wa-ter-ways

board, my boys, she hung up-on the gale;___ on an
neath her bow the fier-y waves she spread,___ and ___
told the strain that held her stout main tack,___ but he

au-tumn night we raised the light on the old head of Kin-sale.
bend-ing low her bos-om of snow, she bur-ied her lee, cat-head.
on-ly laughed as he glanced a loft at a white and sil-v'ry track.

4. The nightly robes our good ship wore were her own topsails three,
Her spanker and her standing jib, the courses being free;
Now lay aloft! my heroes bold, let not a moment pass!
And royals and topgallant sails were quickly on each mast.

5. What looms upon our starboard bow? What hangs upon the breeze?
'Tis time our good ship hauled her wind abreast the old saltee's.
For by her ponderous press of sail and by her escorts four,
We saw our morning visitor was a British man-of-war.

6. Up spoke our noble captain then, and a shot ahead of us passed,
"Haul snug your flowing courses! Lay your topsail to the mast!"
Those Englishmen gave three loud hurrahs from the deck of their covered ark
And we answered back by a solid broadside from the deck of our patriot bark.

7. "Out booms! Out booms!" our skipper cried, "Out booms
        and give her sheet,"
And the swiftest keel that ever was launched shot ahead of the British fleet,
And amidst a thundering shower of shot with the stun-sails hoisting away,
Down the north channel Paul Jones did steer just at the break of day.

JOHNNY HAS GONE FOR A SOLDIER

Soldiers go off to battle, and women live at home in sadness and hope.
During the Revolutionary War those at home sang "Johnny Has Gone for a Soldier."

Slowly, free in delivery

1. —Here I sit on But-ter-milk Hill, who could blame me cry my fill? And ev-'ry tear would turn a mill;

2. I'd sell my clock, I'd sell my reel, like-wise I'd sell my spin-ning wheel to buy my love a sword of steel;

CHORUS:

John-ny has gone for a sol - dier.— Shoo-lie, shoo-lie,
John-ny has gone for a sol - dier.—

shoo - lie__ too, shoo - lie, sac - ca - rac - ca bib - ba - lib - ba boo. If I should die for Sal - ly Bo - bo - link come bib-ba-lib-ba boo sa - ro - ra.

3. Me oh my, I loved him so,
   Broke my heart to see him go,
   And only time will heal my woe;
   Johnny has gone for a soldier.

THE BATTLE OF THE KEGS

The verses are by Francis Hopkinson, who first described the incident to General Washington to the tune of "Yankee Doodle," giving the hard-pressed general one of his few light moments of the war. It is the first record of the use of a floating sea mine.

(*Tune*—YANKEE DOODLE)

1. Gallánts, attend and hear a friend
   Trill forth harmonious ditty;
   Strange things I'll tell which late befell
   In Philadelphia city.

2. 'Twas early day, as poets say,
   Just when the sun was rising,
   A soldier stood on a log of wood
   And saw a thing surprising.

3. As in amaze he stood to gaze,
   The truth can't be deny'd, sir,
   He spy'd a score of kegs or more
   Come floating down the tide, sir.

4. A sailor too in jerkin blue,
   This strange appearance viewing,
   First rubb'd his eyes in great surprise,
   Then said, "Some mischief's brewing."

5. "These kegs, I'm told, the rebels bold
   Packed up like pickling herring,
   And they're come down t'attack the town
   In this new way of ferrying."

6. The soldier flew, the sailor too,
   And scar'd almost to death, sir,
   Wore out their shoes to spread the news
   And ran till out of breath, sir.

7. Now up and down throughout the town
   Most frantic scenes were acted:
   Some ran here and some ran there
   Like men almost distracted.

8. Some fire cry'd, which some deny'd,
   But said the earth had quaked;
   And girls and boys with hideous noise
   Ran through the street half naked.

9. Sir William, he snug as a flea,
   Lay all this time a-snoring,
   Nor dream'd of harm as he lay warm
   In bed with Mrs. Loring.

10. Now in a fright he starts upright,
    Awak'd by such a clatter;
    He rubs both eyes and boldly cries,
    "For God's sake, what's the matter?"

11. At his bedside he then espy'd
    Sir Erskine at command, sir;
    Upon one foot he had one boot
    And th'other in his hand, sir.

12. "Arise, arise," Sir Erskine cries,
    "The rebels, more's the pity,
    Without a boat are all afloat
    And ranged before the city.

13. "The motley crew in vessels new,
    With Satan for their guide, sir,
    Pack'd up in bags or wooden kegs
    Come driving down the tide, sir.

14. "Therefore prepare for bloody war;
    These kegs must all be routed,
    Or surely we'll despised be
    And British courage doubted."

15. The royal band now ready stand,
    All ranged in dread array, sir,
    With stomach stout to see it out
    And make a bloody day, sir.

16. The cannons roar from shore to shore,
    The small arms make a rattle;
    Since wars began I'm sure no man
    E'er saw so strange a battle.

17. The rebel dales, the rebel vales
    With rebel trees surrounded,
    The distant woods, the hills and floods
    With rebel echoes sounded.

18. The fish below swam to and fro,
    Attack'd from every quarter;
    Why sure, thought they, the mischief's
       to pay
    'Mongst folks above the water.

19. The kegs, 'tis said, though strongly
       made
    Of rebel staves and hoops, sir,
    Could not oppose their pow'rful foes:
    The conqu'ring British troops, sir.

20. From morn to night these men of
       might
    Display'd amazing courage,
    And when the sun was fairly down,
    Return'd to sup their porridge.

21. An hundred men with such a pen,
    Or more, upon my word, sir,
    It is most true, would be too few
    Their valor to record, sir.

22. Such feats they did perform that day
    Against those wicked kegs, sir,
    That years to come, if they get home,
    They'll make their boasts and brags,
       sir.

CORNWALLIS COUNTRY DANCE

Burgoyne was defeated at Saratoga, Howe was in Philadelphia, and Cornwallis campaigned in Carolina and Virginia. The retreat and advance of General Cornwallis reminded an American balladeer of the contemporary "cortre" dance, where two facing lines move back and forth.

The English dance tune to which the ballad is set became popular in the early 19th Century Music Halls, as "Pop Goes the Weasel."

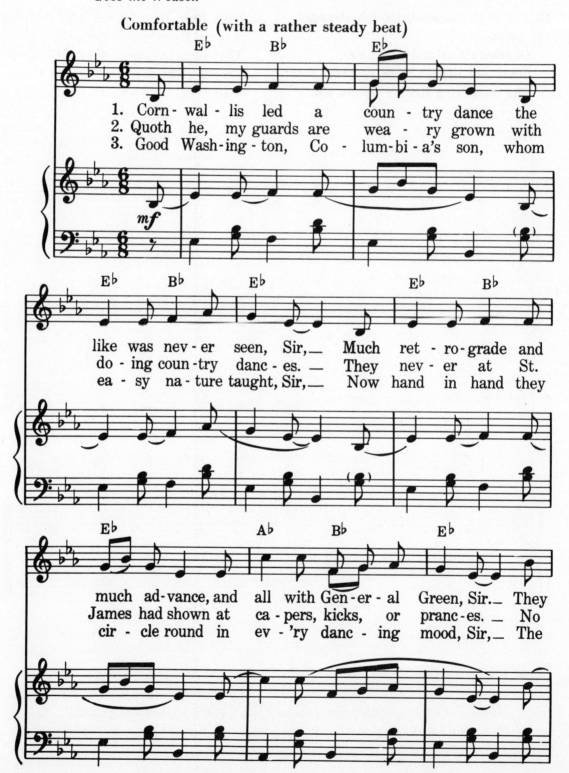

1. Corn - wal - lis led a coun - try dance the like was nev - er seen, Sir,— Much ret - ro - grade and much ad - vance, and all with Gen - er - al Green, Sir.— They

2. Quoth he, my guards are wea - ry grown with do - ing coun - try danc - es. — They nev - er at St. James had shown at ca - pers, kicks, or pranc - es. — No

3. Good Wash - ing - ton, Co - lum - bi - a's son, whom ea - sy na - ture taught, Sir,— Now hand in hand they cir - cle round in ev - 'ry danc - ing mood, Sir,— The

ram - bled up, they ram - bled down, joined hands, and off they
men so gal - lant there were seen while saun - t'ring on pa -
gen - tle move - ment soon con - founds, the Earl's __ day draws

run, Sir, __ of Gen - er - al Green to Charles - town, the
rade, Sir, __ or danc - ing o'er the park so green, or
near, Sir, __ the gen - tle move - ment soon con - founds, the

Earl to Wil - ming - ton, Sir. _____
at the mas - quer - ade, Sir. _____
Earl's __ day draws near, Sir. _____

4. His music soon forgets to play, his feet can't move no more, Sir,
And all his men now curse the day they jigged to our shore, Sir.
Now, Tories all, what can you say . . . Cornwallis is no griper,
But while your hopes are danced away, it's you that pay the piper.

SIR PETER PARKER

Yankee humor found another outlet from the grim reality of fighting in this derisive song. Sir Peter Parker, commanding the British man-of-war Bristol while attacking Charleston, received a heavy cannonading from the rebels. His breeches were torn off and his thigh wounded.

Waltz tempo

1. My Lords, with your leave, an ac-count I will give which de-serves to be writ-ten in me-ter:___ How the reb-els and I___ have been pret-ty

2. With la-bor and toil, un-to Sul-li-van's isle I___ sailed, swift as Fal-staff or Pis-tol,___ but the Yan-kees, dod rat'em, I could-n't get that I

3. Dev-il take 'em, their shot came swift and so hot, and the cow-ard-ly dogs stood so stiff, Sir,___ that I put ship a-bout and was glad to get

nigh, faith, al-most too nigh for Sir Pe-ter! __ Ri
at 'em, so ter-rib-ly mauled my poor Bris-tol.__ Ri
out or they would-n't have left me a skiff, Sir.__ Ri

CHORUS

tu - den di - o, ri tu - den di - ay, Faith,
tu - den di - o, ri tu - den di - ay, so
tu - den di - o, ri tu - den di - ay, or they

al - most too nigh for Sir Pe - ter! _____
ter - rib - ly mauled my poor Bris - tol._____
would-n't have left me a skiff, Sir._____

4. Now Clinton by land did quietly stand,
   While my guns made a terrible rumpus:
   But my pride took a fall when a well-aiméd ball
   Propelled me along on my bumpus!
   Ri tuden dio, ri tuden diay, propelled me along on my bumpus!

5. Now bold as a Turk, I sailed for New York,
   Where with Clinton and Howe you may find me:
   I'd the wind at my tail and I'm hoisting my sail
   To leave Sullivan's Island behind me.
   Ri tuden dio, ri tuden diay, to leave Sullivan's Island behind me!

273

HAIL, COLUMBIA

The aftermath of the Revolutionary War and the birth of the nation is reflected in this song, originally written as "The President's March" for Washington's inauguration in 1789. The words came 10 years later, in 1798, from Judge Joseph Hopkinson in Philadelphia.

With dignity

1. Hail, Co-lum-bia, hap-py land! Hail, ye he-roes
   mor-tal pa-triots, rise once more! De-fend your rights, de-

heav'n-born band! Who fought and bled in Free-dom's cause, Who
fend your shore! Let no rude foe with im-pious hand, Let

fought and bled in Free-dom's cause And when the storm of
no rude foe with im-pious hand, In-vade the shrine where

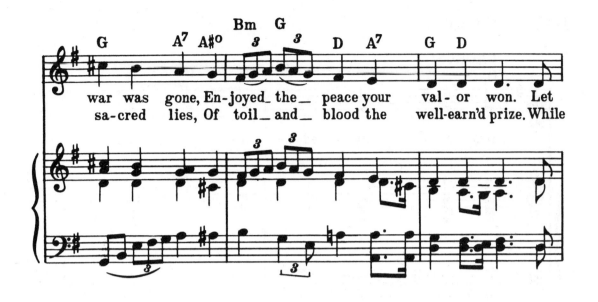

war was gone, En-joyed the peace your val-or won. Let
sa-cred lies, Of toil and blood the well-earn'd prize. While

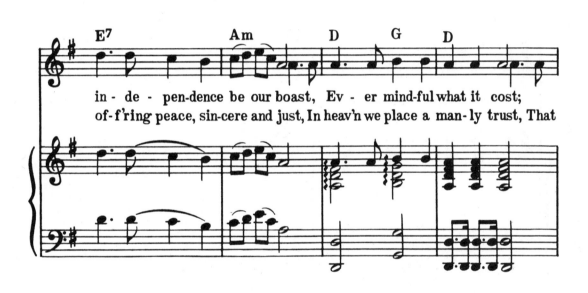

in - de - pen-dence be our boast, Ev - er mind-ful what it cost;
of-f'ring peace, sin-cere and just, In heav'n we place a man-ly trust, That

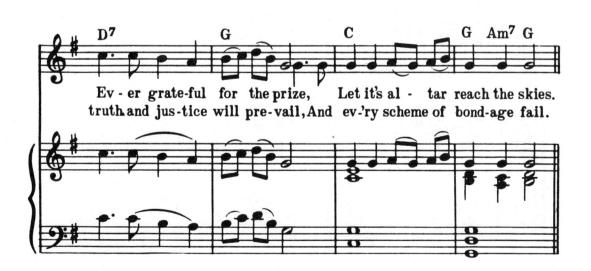

Ev - er grate-ful for the prize, Let it's al - tar reach the skies.
truth and jus-tice will pre-vail, And ev-'ry scheme of bond-age fail.

1812-1850
THE CONSTITUTION AND
THE GUERRIERE

The English and American naval men of the War of 1812 not only were brilliant sailors and fighters but had a sense of personal chivalry and technical rivalry between them. When Captain Dacres surrendered aboard the Constitution, Captain Hull refused to take his sword, took his hat instead, and wore it in his next fight against a British vessel. Years later the two met as friends in Rome.

Free in delivery

1. It oft-times has been told that the
2. The Guer - riere, a frig - ate bold, on the
3. When this frig - ate hove in view, says proud

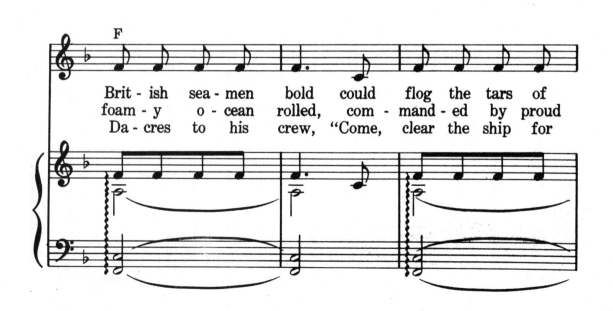

Brit - ish sea - men bold could flog the tars of
foam - y o - cean rolled, com - mand - ed by proud
Da - cres to his crew, "Come, clear the ship for

France so neat and hand-y, oh! __ But they nev-er found their
Da - cres the gran-dee, oh! __ With as choice a Brit - ish
ac - tion and be hand-y, oh! __ To the weath-er gauge, boys,

match till the . Yan-kees they did catch, oh the
crew as a ram-mer ev - er drew, they could
get her," and to make his men fight bet-ter, gave

Yan-kee boys for fight-ing are the dan-dy, oh! ___
flog the French-men two to one so hand-y, oh! ___
them to drink gun-pow-der mixed with bran-dy, oh! ___

4. The British shot flew hot,
   Which the Yankee answered not
   Till they got within the distance they called handy, oh!
   "Now," says Hull unto his crew,
   "Boys, let's see what we can do,
   If we take this boasting Briton, we're the dandy, oh!"

5. The first broadside we poured
   Carried her mainmast by the board,
   Which made this lofty frigate look abandoned, oh!
   Then Dacres shook his head
   And to his officers said,
   "Lord! I didn't think those Yankees were so handy, oh!"

6. Our second told so well
   That their fore and mizzen fell,
   Which doused the royal ensign neat and handy, oh!
   "By George," says he, "we're done."
   And they fired a lee gun
   While the Yankees struck up "Yankee Doodle Dandy," oh!

7. Then Dacres came on board
   To deliver up his sword;
   Loath was he to part with it, it was so handy, oh!
   "Oh, keep your sword," says Hull,
   For it only makes you dull;
   Cheer up and let's have a little brandy, oh!"

YE PARLIAMENTS OF ENGLAND

This song is a nice summary of American hopes in mid-war, 1812. Perry had recouped American losses on Lake Erie (and in the last stanza, the song writer thought it possible for us to acquire Canada). This was before Napoleon's capture freed the British fleets and troops for the landing in America that led to the burning of Washington, D.C.

In 2, like a march

1. Ye par-lia-ments of Eng-land, ye Lords and Com-mons,
2. You first con-fined our com-merce: you said our ships shan't

too,___ con - sid - er well what you're a - bout, and
trade,___ and then im-pressed our sea - men, and

what you're goin' to do:___ you're now at war with
used them as your slaves;___ you then in-sult - ed

Yan - kees, and I'm sure you'll rue the day __ you
Rodg - ers while sail - ing on the main, __ and

roused the sons of Lib - er - ty in North A - mer - i - cay __
had we not de - clar - èd war, you'd done it o'er a - gain. __

r.h.

3. You thought our frigates were but few and Yankees could not fight,
   Until brave Hull your Guerrière took and banished her from sight.
   You're now at war with Yankees; I'm sure you'll rue the day
   You roused the sons of liberty in North Americay.

4. Soon upon Lake Erie, bold Perry had his fun;
   You own he beat your naval force and caused them all to run;
   While Chauncey on Ontario, the like known ne'er before,
   Your British squadron beat complete: some took, some run ashore.

5. Use every endeavor to try to cause a peace,
   For Yankee ships are building fast, their navy to increase.
   They will enforce their commerce; their laws by heaven were made,
   That Yankee ships in time of peace in any port might trade.

6. Grant us free trade and commerce, don't you impress our men,
   Give up all claims to Canada, then we'll make peace again.
   Then, England, we'll respect you and treat you as a friend;
   Respect our flag and citizens, then all these wars will end.

PATRIOTIC DIGGERS

Free Americans from all walks of life rose in de-fense of their new nation. This war song was in-spired by Samuel Woodward, who wrote the "Old Oaken Bucket" and other songs.

Medium, in 2

1. En-e-mies, be-ware,   keep a prop-er dis-tance,
   To pro-tect our rights   'gainst your flint and trig-gers
2. Schol-ars leave their schools with pa-tri-ot-ic teach-ers,
   Bright A-pol-lo's sons   leave their pipe and ta-bor,

else we'll make you stare   at our firm re-sis-tance;
see on yon-der heights our   pa-tri-ot-ic dig-gers.
farm-ers seize their tools,   head-ed by their preach-ers,
mid the roar of   guns   join the mar-tial la-bor,

let a-lone the lads   who are free-dom tast-ing,
Men of ev-'ry age,   col-or, rank, pro-fes-sion,
how they break the soil —   brew-ers, butch-ers, bak-ers —
round the em-bat-tled plain   in sweet con-cord ral-ly,

don't for-get, our dads gave you once a bast-ing.
ar -dent-ly en - gaged, la - bor in suc - ces - sion.
here the doc-tors toil, there the un-der-tak-ers.
and in free-dom's strain sing the foe's fi - na - le.

CHORUS:

Pick-axe, shov-el, spade, crow-bar, hoe, and bar-row,

bet-ter not in - vade, Yan-kees have the mar-row.

3. Better not invade, don't forget the spirit
Which our dads displayed and their sons inherit.
If you still advance, friendly caution slighting,
You may get by chance a bellyful of fighting!
Plumbers, founders, dyers, tinmen, turners, shavers,
Sweepers, clerks, and criers, jewelers and engravers,
Clothiers, drapers, players, cartmen, hatters, tailors,
Gaugers, sealers, weighers, carpenters and sailors!

Chorus

THE HUNTERS OF KENTUCKY

Jackson and his brave Kentuckians fought the battle of New Orleans two weeks after the war was over, because communication was so slow that they didn't know the peace was signed.

This song was written by Samuel Woodward in 1830, using the melody of an English Music Hall song, "Miss Bailey's Ghost."

1. Ye gen-tle-men and la-dies fair, Who grace this fam-ous
2. We are a hard-y, free-born race, Each man to fear a

cit-y, ___ Just lis-ten if you've time to spare, While
stran-ger; ___ What-e'er the game we'll join the chase, De-

I re-hearse a dit-ty; ___ And for the op-por-
spoil-ing time and dan-ger, ___ And if the dar-ing

tun- i - ty, Con- ceive your-selves quite luck-y, ___ For
foe an-noys, What- e'er his strength and forc-es, ___ We'll

'tis not oft-en that you see A hun-ter from Ken-tuck-y. __
show him that Ken-tuck-y boys Are al- li- ga- tor hors-es.__

CHORUS:

Oh Ken-tuck-y, the hun-ters of Ken-tuck-y! tuck-y!

3. You've heard, I s'pose, how New Orleans
   Is famed for wealth and beauty;
   There's girls of every hue, it seems,
   From snowy white to sooty.
   So Pakenham, he made his brags,
   If he in fight was lucky,
   He'd have their girls and cotton bags,
   In spite of old Kentucky.
   Chorus

4. But Jackson, he was wide awake
   And was not scar'd at trifles,
   For well he knew what aim we take
   With old Kentucky rifles.
   So he led us down the cypress swamp,
   The ground was low and mucky;
   There stood John Bull in martial pomp
   And here was old Kentucky.
   Chorus

THE HORNET AND THE PEACOCK

The victory of the American Hornet *over the British frigate* Peacock *greatly cheered an American public, gloomy after many land reverses. Later the Hornet barely got away from the 74-gun* Cornwallis *by throwing overboard all guns, lifeboats, and other movable objects.*

With command (free in delivery)

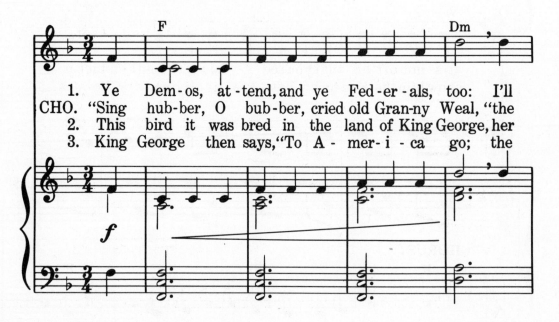

1. Ye Dem-os, at-tend, and ye Fed-er-als, too: I'll
CHO. "Sing hub-ber, O bub-ber, cried old Gran-ny Weal, "the
2. This bird it was bred in the land of King George, her
3. King George then says, "To A-mer-i-ca go; the

sing you a song that you all know is true, con-
Hor-net can tick-le the Brit-ish bird's tail! Her
feath-ers were fine and her tail ver-y large: she
Hor-net, the Wasp, is the Brit-ish king's foe: Pick them

cern-ing the Hor-net, true stuff, I'll be bail, that
stings are all sharp, and they'll pierce with-out fail; suc -
spread forth her wings, like a ship in full sail, and
up, my dear bird, spread your wings to the gale." "But be-

rum-pled the Pea-cock and low-ered her tail.
cess to our na - vy!" cried old Gran-ny Weal.
prid - ed her - self in the size of her tail. (repeat Cho.)
ware of these in-sects," cries old Gran-ny Weal. (repeat Cho.)

4. Away flew this bird at the word of command,
   Her flight was directed to freedom's own land;
   The Hornet discovered her wings on the sail,
   And quickly determined to tickle her tail. *Chorus*

5. So at it they went, it was both pick and stick,
   The Hornet still working keen under her wing;
   "American insects," quoth she, "I'll be bail,
   Will humble the king bird and tickle her tail." *Chorus*

6. The Peacock now mortally under her wing
   Did feel the full force of the Hornet's sharp sting;
   She flattened her crest like a shoal on the whale,
   Sunk down by her side and lower'd her tail. *Chorus*

7. Success to brave Lawrence, who well knew the nest
   Where the Hornet and Wasp with honor still rest.
   We'll send them a force, and with skill, I'll be bail,
   Will humble King George and tickle his tail. *Chorus*

287

1850-1898
THE ABOLITIONIST HYMN

With rising feeling over the slavery issue, the New England churches began singing secular hymns against slavery much as they sang hymns against the British during the Revolution. This popular anti-slavery hymn was sung to the hymn melody familiar since Colonial days, of "Old Hundred."

Definite, but not too slow

1. We ask not that the slave should lie as lies his master: at his ease, beneath a silk-en can-o-py, or in the shade of bloom-ing trees.
2. We ask not "eye for eye" that all who forge the chain and ply the whip should feel their tor-ture, while the thrall should wield the scourge of mas-ter-ship.
3. We mourn not that the man should toil: 'tis Na-ture's need, 'tis God's de-cree; but let the hand that tills the soil be, like the wind that fans it, free.

JOHN BROWN

There have been innumerable versions and parodies of this song, whose melody formed the basis for Julia Ward Howe's "Battle Hymn of the Republic" and the famous parody, "John Brown's Body Lies A-Moulderin' in the Grave." The version reproduced here was one sung in churches around the land.

Stirring march

1. John Brown died on the scaf-fold for the slave!
2. John Brown sowed and the har-vest-ers are we;

Dark was the hour when we dug his hal-lowed grave;
Hon - or to him who has made the bonds-man free;

Now God a - veng - es the life he glad - ly gave,
Loved ev - er-more shall this, our no-ble lead - er be,

JOHN BROWN

Free - dom   reigns to - day!_____
Free - dom   reigns to - day!_____

CHORUS:

Glo - ry, glo - ry, hal - le - lu - jah!

Glo - ry, glo - ry, hal - le - lu - jah!

Glo - ry, glo - ry, hal - le - lu - jah!

Free - dom reigns to - day.____

3. John Brown's body lies mouldering in the grave;
   Bright o'er the sod let the starry banner wave;
   Lo, for the millions he periled all to save,
   Freedom reigns today!
   Chorus

4. John Brown lives, we are gaining on our foes;
   Right shall be victor whatever may oppose;
   Fresh through the darkness the wind of morning blows;
   Freedom reigns today!

5. John Brown's soul through the world is marching on;
   Hail to the hour when oppression shall be gone;
   All men will sing in the better day's dawn:
   Freedom reigns today!

6. John Brown dwells where the battle's strife is o'er;
   Hate cannot harm him, nor sorrow stir him more;
   Earth will remember the martyrdom he bore;
   Freedom reigns today!

7. John Brown's body lies mouldering in the grave;
   John Brown lives in the triumphs of the brave;
   John Brown's soul not a higher joy can crave:
   Freedom reigns today!

NOBODY KNOWS THE TROUBLE I'VE SEEN

The North knew little about Southern Negro music until after 1871, when the Fiske University Jubilee Singers made their concert tour. Here is one of the many songs they made popular here and abroad. It is not only an exquisite example of the Negro spiritual, but sets the atmosphere of pre-Civil War.

Free in delivery

The end

CHORUS:

1. Some-times I'm up, Some-times I'm down,
2. What makes old Sa-tan hate me so,

Oh yes, Lord! Some-times I'm al-most
Oh yes, Lord! He got me once and he

to the ground, Oh yes, Lord!
let me go, Oh yes, Lord!

BATTLE CRY OF FREEDOM

(RALLYING SONG)

The original words (see following page) and music were composed during the Civil War by George Root, a great song writer of the mid-nineteenth century, composer of "Just Before the Battle, Mother," "The Vacant Chair," and many others. It was popular as a marching song and became this rallying song for the Spanish-American War.

Lusty march

1. Yes, we'll ral - ly 'round the flag, boys, we'll ral - ly once a-
2. We are spring-ing to the call of our broth-ers gone be-

gain,   Shout - ing the bat - tle cry of free - -
fore,   Shout - ing the bat - tle cry of free - -

dom;   We will ral - ly from the hill - side, we'll gath - er from the
dom;   And we'll fill the va - cant ranks with a mil - lion free-men

Shout - ing the bat - tle cry of free - - - dom.__

3. We will welcome to our numbers the loyal, true and brave,
   Shouting the battle cry of freedom,
   And altho' they may be poor, not a man shall be a slave,
   Shouting the battle cry of freedom. *Chorus*

4. So we're springing to the call from the East and from the West,
   Shouting the battle cry of freedom,
   And we'll hurl the rebel crew from the land we love the best,
   Shouting the battle cry of freedom. *Chorus*

THE BATTLE CRY OF FREEDOM
(CIVIL WAR BATTLE SONG)

1. We are marching to the fields, boys, we're going to the fight,
   Shouting the battle cry of freedom;
   And we bear the glorious stars for the Union and the right,
   Shouting the battle cry of freedom.
   Chorus: The Union forever, hurrah, boys, hurrah!
   Down with the traitor, up with the stars;
   For we're marching to the field, boys, going to the fight,
   Shouting the battle cry of freedom!

2. We will meet the rebel host, boys, with fearless hearts and true,
   Shouting the battle cry of freedom;
   And we'll show what Uncle Sam has for loyal men to do,
   Shouting the battle cry of freedom. *Chorus*

3. If we fall amid the fray, boys, we'll face them to the last,
   Shouting the battle cry of freedom,
   And our comrades brave shall hear us as they go rushing past,
   Shouting the battle cry of freedom. *Chorus*

4. Yes, for Liberty and Union we're springing to the fight,
   Shouting the battle cry of freedom;
   And the vic'try shall be ours, for we're rising in our might,
   Shouting the battle cry of freedom. *Chorus*

THE BATTLE CRY OF FREEDOM

(*Civil War Parody:* MARY HAD A LITTLE LAMB)

Mary had a little lamb,
'Twas always on the go,
Shouting the battle cry of freedom.
So she staked it on a grassy slope
Along the Shenando',
Shouting the battle cry of freedom.
Chorus: Hurrah for Mary! Hurrah for the lamb!
　　　　　Hurrah for the sojers, who didn't care a damn,
　　　　　For we'll rally round the flag, boys,
　　　　　We'll rally once again,
　　　　　Shouting the battle cry of freedom.

And frequently she turned it loose
Upon the bank to play,
Shouting the battle cry of freedom.
The sojers eyed it from the shore
In a kleptomaniac way,
Shouting the battle cry of freedom.
Chorus

"What makes the men love mutton so?"
The colonel he did cry,
Shouting the battle cry of freedom.
"Cause mutton makes the whiskers grow,"
The sojers did reply,
Shouting the battle cry of freedom.
Chorus

It swam across the Shenando',
Our pickets saw it too,
Shouting the battle cry of freedom.
And speedily it simmered down
Into a mutton stew,
Shouting the battle cry of freedom.
Chorus

And Mary never more did see
Her darling little lamb,
Shouting the battle cry of freedom.
For the boys in blue they chawed it up
And didn't give a damn,
Shouting the battle cry of freedom.
Chorus

THE BONNIE BLUE FLAG

*The excellent music of an Irish variety hall tune,
"The Irish Jaunting Car," was put to patriotic use
by the Irish comedian, Henry McCarthy. In the
South it was surpassed in popularity only by "Dixie."*

With a gay lilt

1. We are a band of broth-ers,— and
2. As long as the Un-ion— was

na-tive to the soil, Fight-ing for the
faith-ful to her trust,— Like friends and like

prop-er-ty we gained by hon-est toil;— And
broth-ers,— Kind were we and just.— But

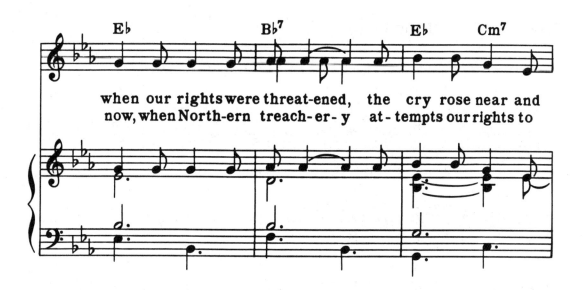

when our rights were threat-ened, the cry rose near and
now, when North-ern treach-er-y at-tempts our rights to

far:___ "Hur- rah for the Bon-nie Blue Flag that
mar,___ We hoist on high the Bon-nie Blue Flag that

bears a sin - gle star!"___ Hur - rah!___ Hur-
bears a sin - gle star!___ Hur - rah!___ Hur-

rah! __ For South-ern rights, hur- rah! __ Hur- rah for the

Bon-nie Blue Flag that bears a sin- gle star! __

GOOBER PEAS

Armies must march and soldiers will gripe. Food was a problem to the Confederate Army in the war between the States. Peanuts (goober peas) grow easily in the South, and became a wry joke to the Confederate soldier when he could find nothing else to eat.

With a jolly lilt

1. Sit - ting by the road - side on a sum-mer's day, Chat - ting with my mess - mates, pass - ing time a - way. Ly - ing in the
2. When a horse-man pass - es, The sol-diers have a rule, Cry out at their loud - est,— "Mis - ter, here's your mule!" But an-oth - er

GOOBER PEAS

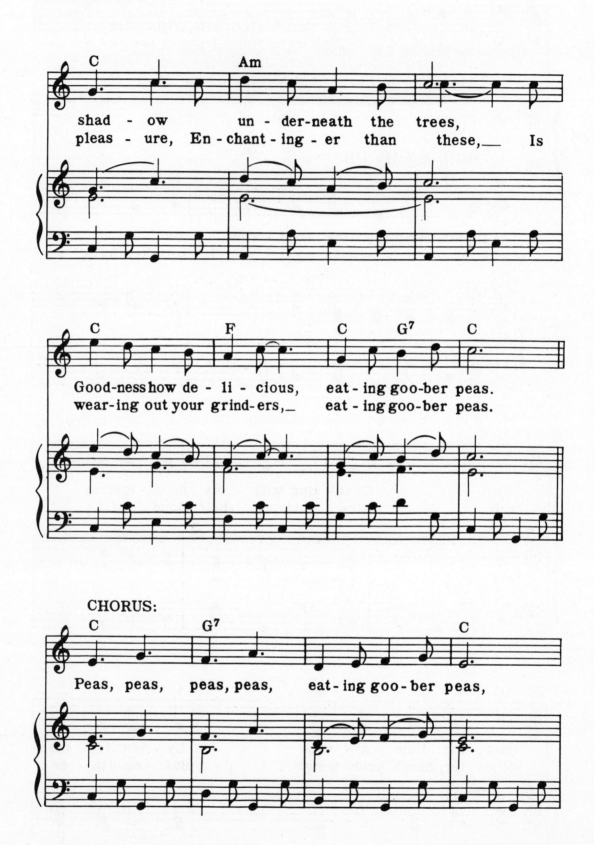

shad - ow   un - der-neath the   trees,
pleas - ure, En - chant - ing - er   than   these,___ Is

Good-ness how de - li - cious,   eat - ing goo-ber peas.
wear-ing out your grind-ers,___   eat - ing goo-ber peas.

CHORUS:

Peas, peas,   peas, peas,   eat - ing goo - ber peas,

Good-ness how de - li - cious, eat-ing goo-ber peas. ___

3. Just before the battle, the general hears a row;
   He says, "The Yanks are comin', I hear their rifles now."
   He turns around in wonder, and what do you think he sees?
   The Georgia Militia eating goober peas.
   Chorus

4. I think my song has lasted almost long enough;
   The subject's interesting, but the rhymes are getting tough;
   I wish this war was over, and free from rags and fleas,
   We'd kiss our wives and sweethearts and gobble goober peas.
   Chorus

ALL QUIET ALONG THE POTOMAC

In the early days of the war, North and South were stalemated on opposite sides of the Potomac River. A catch phrase of the time was "All Quiet Along the Potomac."

With soft rhythm

1. "All qui-et a-long the Po-to-mac to-night," Ex-cept here and there a stray pick-et ___ Is shot as he walks on his beat to and

2. "All qui-et a-long the Po-to-mac to-night," There the sol-diers lie peace-ful-ly dream-ing. ___ And their tents in the rays of the clear, au-tumn

fro, By a ri - fle-man hid in the thick- et.
moon And the rays of the camp-fires are gleam-ing.

'Tis noth - ing, a pri - vate or two now and
A trem - u-lous sigh as the gen - tle, night

then Will not count in the news of the bat - tle.
wind Through the for - est leaves slow - ly is creep-ing.

ALL QUIET ALONG THE POTOMAC

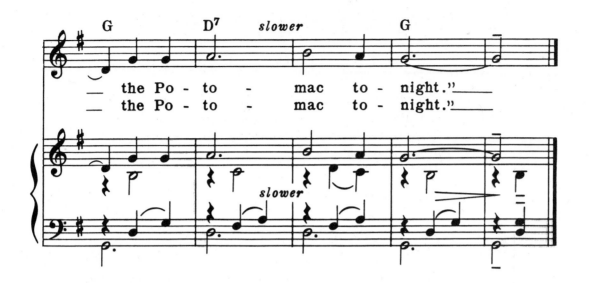

the Po - to - mac to - night."

the Po - to - mac to - night."

3. Hark! Was it the night wind that rustled the leaves?
   Was it the moonlight so wondrously flashing?
   It looked like a rifle! "Ha! Mary, good-bye!"
   And his life-blood is ebbing and plashing.

4. "All quiet along the Potomac tonight."
   No sound save the sound of the river,
   While soft falls the dew on the face of the dead;
   The picket's off duty forever.
   "All quiet along the Potomac tonight."

WHEN JOHNNY COMES
MARCHING HOME

*The Bandmaster of the Union Army, Patrick Gil-
more, adapted a rousing old English folk song "The
Three Crows," which soldiers and civilians sang all
through the Civil War...*

men will cheer,___ the boys will shout, The
vil - lage lads___ and las - sies say, With

la - dies they will all turn out, And we'll all feel
ros - es they will strew the way,

gay when John - ny comes march-ing home.___

3. Get ready for the Jubilee,
   Hurrah! Hurrah!
   We'll give the hero three times three,
   Hurrah! Hurrah!
   The laurel wreath is ready now
   To place upon his loyal brow,
   And we'll all feel gay
   When Johnny comes marching home.

4. In eighteen hundred and sixty-one,
   Hurrah! Hurrah!
   That was when the war begun,
   Hurrah! Hurrah!
   In eighteen hundred and sixty-two
   Both sides were falling to,
   And we'll all drink stone wine
   When Johnny comes marching home.

5. In eighteen hundred and sixty-four,
   Hurrah! Hurrah!
   Abe called for five hundred thousand more,
   Hurrah! Hurrah!
   In eighteen hundred and sixty-five
   They talked rebellion—strife
   And we'll all drink stone wine
   When Johnny comes marching home.

THE BATTLE OF BULL RUN

(SOUTHERN VERSION)

To the tune of "When Johnny Comes Marching Home" the Southern soldiers sang these verses, and the Yankees made up their answer.

3. In eighteen hundred and sixty-three
   "Skugaugh," says I;
   In eighteen hundred and sixty-three,
   You ought to seen them Yankees flee;
   Chorus

4. In eighteen hundred and sixty-four,
   "Skugaugh," says I;
   In eighteen hundred and sixty-four
   Them Yankees cried, "We want no more."
   Chorus

5. In eighteen hundred and sixty-five,
   "Skugaugh," says I;
   In eighteen hundred and sixty-five
   We all thanked God we were alive.
   Chorus

NORTHERN VERSION

From across the lines, the Southerners could hear the Yankees sing the same song.

Through a mistake we lost Bull Run,
"Three balls," says I;
Through a mistake we lost Bull Run,
"Three balls," says I;
Through a mistake we lost Bull Run
And we all skedaddled to Washington,
And we'll all drink stone blind,
Johnny come fill the bowl.

AMERICA THE BEAUTIFUL

Written by Katharine Lee Bates when she was Professor of English at Wellesley College, to the old hymn tune, "Materia," these extraordinarily beautiful words are seldom listened to. They deserve much more attention, as one expression of what Americans feel for their land and why.

With dignity - in 4

1. O beau-ti-ful for spa-cious skies, For am-ber waves of grain, For pur-ple moun-tain maj-es-ties A-bove the fruit-ed plain! A-mer-i-ca! A-mer-i-ca! God

2. O beau-ti-ful for pil-grim feet Whose stern im-pas-sion'd stress A thor-ough-fare for free-dom beat A-cross the wil-der-ness! A-mer-i-ca! A-mer-i-ca! God

shed His grace on thee, And crown thy good with
mend thine ev-'ry flaw, Con-firm thy soul in

broth-er-hood, From sea to shin-ing sea!
self-con-trol, Thy lib-er-ty in law!

3. O beautiful for heroes proved
   In liberating strife,
   Who more than self their country loved,
   And mercy more than life!
   America! America!
   May God thy gold refine,
   Till all success be nobleness,
   And every gain divine!

4. O beautiful for patriot dream
   That sees beyond the years;
   Thine alabaster cities gleam
   Undimmed by human tears!
   America! America!
   God shed His grace on thee,
   And crown thy good with brotherhood
   From sea to shining sea!